T0151390

CURING JAPAN'S AMERICA ADDICTION

CUR

ING

"THE PROUD JAPANESE ACCOMPLISHMENT

JAP

AN'S

KNOWN AS THE MASSIVE MIDDLE-CLASS

AME

RICA HAS BEEN DESTROYED,

ADDI

TION

AND THAT IS THE LEGACY OF THE KOIZUMI REFORMS."

MO

ITA

SUMMER 2008
CHIN MUSIC PRESS, PUBLISHERS
SEATTLE — TOKYO

kami
PAPERBACK
SERIES

COPYRIGHT
by Minoru Morita

—

TRANSLATION COPYRIGHT
by Bruce Rutledge
& Yuko Enomoto

—

CHIN MUSIC PRESS INC.
2621 24th Ave W
Seattle WA 98199–3407
USA

—

WEB ACCESS
http://chinmusicpress.com

—

SUMMER 2008
First edition

—

INTERIOR AND COVER DESIGN
by Craig Mod

—

PRINTED & BOUND
in Japan *by* Yushin Printing

—

LIBRARY OF CONGRESS CATALOGING-IN-PUBLICATION DATA
Morita, Minoru
Curing Japan's America Addiction
By Minoru Morita;
translated by Bruce Rutledge & Yuko Enomoto;
designed by Craig Mod;
edited by Bruce & David Rutledge

—

ISBN 978-0974-1995-42

—

1. Politics 2. Japan Studies

This translation is dedicated to Hiroshi "Day" Inoshita,
a great teacher and friend

TABLE OF
CONTENTS

The **Addiction**

The **Diagnosis**

The **Cure**

A MESSAGE
TO MY AMERICAN READERS

Dear readers,

I am Minoru Morita, a Japanese political analyst. I also preside over the Morita Juku, a Japanese institute of learning. I was born on October 23, 1932, in a town called Ito in Shizuoka Prefecture, right near Mount Fuji. That makes me seventy-five years old today. When World War II came to an end in 1945, I was in the first year of middle school. My minimal war experience amounts to a few short months serving in the Japanese military. I've lived sixty-three of my years in this postwar age. And fifty years ago, I began working as a journalist.

The starting point for Japan after the war was a pledge never to wage war again. Before World War II broke out, the Japanese government — and the greater Japanese empire — committed a grave offense by going to war. Once that war was over, the Japanese people swore they would never fight in another war again. Instead, we chose to live in an amicable fashion.

During the sixty-three years since the war ended, Japan has lived under the shadow of the United States. Japan has experienced prosperity and decline during this time. The majority of Japanese people like Americans. We hope to always have friendly relations with the US. At the same time, in Japan today, there is a welling up of animosity toward the American government. I want my American readers especially to know this. If the Japanese and Americans are to live together amiably, we need to truly understand each other.

I wanted to publish this book in English so that the American people would understand Japanese politics. For making this possible, I would like to express my deep gratitude to Bruce Rutledge and Yuko Enomoto.

MINORU MORITA
Political analyst
President, Mirota Juku
April 28, 2008
(The fifty-sixth anniversary of
Japan's independence)

まえがき————————————

アメリカの読者の皆さんへの
メッセージ

政治評論家・森田塾塾長　　森田 実

アメリカの読者の皆さん。私は日本の政治評論家の森田実と申します。森田塾という教育組織を主宰しています。1932年10月23日、富士山の近くの静岡県伊東市に生まれました。ただいま75歳です。第2次世界大戦が終わった1945年当時、私は中学1年生でした。ほんの数カ月間ですが、日本軍人の指揮下で労働に従事しました。最年少の戦争体験です。それから戦後の63年間、時代とともに生きてきました。50年前からはジャーナリストとして働いてきました。

戦後の日本の原点は再び戦争をしないことにあります。第2次大戦前の日本政府すなわち大日本帝国は戦争をするという大きな過ちを犯しました。戦争が終わったとき、日本国民は再び戦争をしないことを誓いました。日本国民は友好的に生きることを希望しています。

戦後63年間、日本はアメリカの影響下で生きてきました。繁栄も衰退も体験しました。大多数の日本国民はアメリカ国民が好きです。アメリカ国民と未来永劫友好関係のなかで生きていきたいと望んでいます。同時に、最近日本国民のなかにアメリカ政府への不信が拡大しています。このことも知っていただきたいと思います。日米両国民が信頼し合うためには正しい相互理解が必要です。

アメリカ国民の皆さんに日本の政治を理解していただきたいと念願して、本書をアメリカにおいて出版していただくことにしました。出版にあたり大変お世話になったブルース・ラトレッジさんと榎本夕子さんに深く感謝いたします。

2008.4.28　56年前日本が独立した日に

TRANSLATOR'S NOTE

In November 2006, reporter Takehiko Kambayashi took me aside at a party in Tokyo and asked if I'd be interested in translating the work of Minoru Morita. It was an easy question to answer. During my years reporting and editing in Japan, I enjoyed Morita's insightful, no-nonsense style of political commentary. He doesn't pander to his audience and he also doesn't worry too much about stepping on a few toes. He breaks the myth of the pacifist being timid and cowardly. Morita's brand of pacifism is fiery and insistent. He suffers no fools. That appealed to me.

Since late 2006, Yuko Enomoto and I have been translating Morita's weekly columns. The more we translated them, the more I felt that I was looking at the left's response to the famous right-wing tome of 1991, Shintaro Ishihara's *The Japan That Can Say No*. In *Curing Japan's America Addiction*, Morita's first work translated into English, the author also urges Japan to stand up and say "no" to the US, but this time it's for reasons that make sense. This is not an author stepping up on the Japan as No. 1 bandwagon; it's an author urging the Japanese to say no to their addiction to the US because the relationship has turned destructive. For that reason, I think this is an important work for understanding contemporary Japan and the changing dynamics of the US-Japan relationship.

Yuko and I have loved working with Mr. Morita. His prose is straightforward and erudite, often a difficult combination for writers to achieve. He is gracious to a fault and a delight to work with. Our sincere wish is that this translated version of his work gives an inkling of his colorful, sharp and insightful style.

We also want to thank Takehiko Kambayashi, whose reporting brought to life the views of the ordinary Japanese in these pages. Without his efforts, this book never would have been made.

BRUCE RUTLEDGE
Seattle
April 28, 2008

Note on the text: The glossary replaces footnotes and indexes in this edition, defining highlighted terms and names in the order that they appear in the book.

Man is but a reed,
the most feeble thing in nature,
but he is a thinking reed.

— BLAISE PASCAL, PENSEES (#347)

The Addiction

CHAPTER 1

MODERN JAPAN: MADE FOR AMERI

I BELIEVE THAT JAPANESE POLITICS IS ON THE VERGE OF THE greatest crisis in its history. Japanese politicians have forgotten their sense of political duty. We have trouble acknowledging the steady decline of political morality in Japan because we've forgotten the sage advice of nineteenth century English politician William E. Gladstone: "It is the duty of government to make it difficult for people to do wrong, easy to do right."

Japanese politicians have made serving the American government a priority when they should be focused on serving the Japanese people. Japan has lost its sovereignty to the United States. Our nation has been invaded and occupied by invisible forces.

Japan's economy is vulnerable.

Executives in Japan's leading corporations are increasingly focused solely on profit, and any sense of corporate responsibility to

Japanese society is all but forgotten. While corporate players should be pursuing economic activities that improve the livelihoods of all Japanese people, they have come down with a case of me-ism. Take care of yourself and to hell with the rest, the thinking goes.

Even the intense passion and sense of responsibility once exercised by the leaders of our financial institutions and governmental organizations is in rapid decline. The financial elite have all but forgotten their sense of fairness and responsibility toward the Japanese

N CONSUMPTION

people, and governmental organizations have lost their sense of independence. That independent spirit has been replaced by a single-minded focus on the priorities of Japan's coalition government and the government of the United States.

The degeneration of Japan's mass media—with national newspapers and TV stations at the center—has been difficult to watch. The media has discarded its sense of independence and objectivity in the face of political power. Major news organizations have abandoned their normal skepticism, instead choosing to enlist as the public relations arm of the government. Most of the journalists working for these organizations have lost the spirit of journalism, which is about digging for the truth.

Even Japan's administration of justice, which should be the last bastion in the separation of powers, has lost its way and now primarily serves the political powers that be.

There is a well-known saying by Chinese philosopher Mencius: "The people are the most important element in a nation; the spirits of the land and grain come next; the sovereign counts for the least." Our political leaders should take these words to heart, but unfortunately, this sort of thinking has greatly declined among today's leaders.

We can't let this situation fester any longer.

We must stop the anti-Japanese, pro-US, extreme right-wing government we have now and create a more benevolent government. Japanese citizens are the only ones who can make this happen. The only way to stop this government from recklessly barreling down its present path is to vote it out of office.

Thinking Reeds

Blaise Pascal wrote that "man is but a reed, the most feeble thing in nature; but he is a thinking reed." Now is the time for the Japanese people to become like Pascal's thinking reeds and set the country free.

The Japanese must become thinking reeds. Even if we are just weak beings by ourselves, if many of us can move in unity, I believe we can rid ourselves of the bad elements in the political world who would do us harm.

I believe this applies to the good people of the United States too. The reason I wrote this book is to challenge you to become "thinking reeds."

What is happening in Japan? At this moment in history, we need to know the truth. We can't allow ourselves to settle for the half-truths reported by the mass media; we can't just be satisfied knowing the surface of things. We must begin to see what is happening economically and socially in Japan. First and foremost, we must understand that Japan is ruled by the American government and its largest investors.

Japan's national television stations and major newspapers cover the country's politics based on a lie: They treat Japan like an independent nation. Many Japanese people believe in this lie. But what is the truth? Isn't the Japanese government more like a Japanese branch of the American government? While Japan, the junior ally, protects its big boss, the wealth of the Japanese is being sucked up by the American government and the largest American investment funds. It's as if Japan were made for American consumption.

The time has come for us to check and double-check what we hear from politicians and the mass media. We can't allow ourselves to be fooled or to give our consent to what we don't understand. We need to listen carefully and confirm what we hear. We just can't keep swallowing the messages from the mass media anymore. When we have questions, we should work to find the answers. Japan needs a national debate. Then the Japanese people can express their intentions by the ballot box.

This is the age of elections, and the coming elections are connected to the consciousness of the Japanese people. If they begin to realize who they are, they can correct the current political path, and they can begin to rebuild this nation as a truly independent one.

On these pages, you'll find the truth about Japan and you'll glimpse the light at the end of the tunnel if we can get Japanese politics to head toward the proper goals.

Written in March 2007, four months before the opposition took control of the upper house for the first time since World War II.

CHAPTER 2

THE UNBEARABLE BURDEN OF KOIZUMI'S

REMEMBER THE SHORT, BRUTISH POLITICAL LIFE OF former Prime Minister **Shinzo Abe**, the man who took over when **Junichiro Koizumi** stepped down in late summer 2006? Around the end of that year, there were whispers in the halls of Nagatacho—the Tokyo neighborhood where Japan's central government is located—that Abe and his cabinet were about to resign. By early 2007, several opinion polls showed support for his administration plummeting from 65% when he took office in September 2006 to as low as 40%. Why did Abe's approval ratings drop so far in such a short time?

The reason was that Abe went around talking about how he was Koizumi's successor and he would continue Koizumi's policies. This was not the way to rebuild Japan, and the voters knew it.

A large number of Japanese people are suffering from the legacy of

Koizumi's term—a long five years and five months that began in April 2001 and extended until September 2006, when Abe stepped in.

The so-called **Koizumi Revolution** brought to Japan a form of extreme market fundamentalism that is crushing the country. It left the Japanese people poorer and it mercilessly abandoned the outlying provinces. Many of the smallest Japanese companies were pushed into bankruptcy, and the country's wealth gap widened. This is the reality of the Koizumi Revolution so heralded in the West.

EVOLUTION

Koizumi politics destroyed Japan's egalitarian, middle-class society, lined the pockets of a few and left the far bigger majority poorer. And the whole time, the Koizumi administration was being manipulated by the US administration of George W. Bush.

It was the Koizumi administration that decided to Americanize Japan and create a destructive wealth gap, but it was the Bush administration that was providing the instructions. Along the way, they had a lot of help from politicians in the ruling coalition, elite bureaucrats in the central government, economic leaders, academics and journalists who practically worship the US. To properly rebuild Japan, we have to recognize this truth.

Let's not mince words: Prime Minister Koizumi was the worst and most frivolous sort of puppet politician that Japan has seen since World War II. He's seen as a good guy, but he is behind the degeneration of politics and the corruption of the media. The damage he has done needs to be fixed as quickly as possible.

As soon as Abe took power, the burden of inheriting Koizumi's revolution was apparent. The wealth gap continued to grow, more people became poorer, the outlying provinces began to wither, the medical system teetered, the education system became flimsier ... the list goes on and on.

The Koizumi administration's mishandling of the government has led to a new class of people who work diligently but can barely make ends meet. They are Japan's working poor. Of the fifty-five million or so workers in Japan, about 15% are said to fit this description. Japan has turned itself into a horribly dark society.

When former Prime Minister Abe appeared on the scene, his only chance to win the support of the Japanese people was to reverse course with all the political will he could muster. To save the badly damaged Japanese nation, he needed to repudiate the Koizumi legacy and begin to rebuild Japan with new policies.

But of course—as we all know now—Abe couldn't do that. After all, he became prime minister because of Koizumi's support and thus, he couldn't escape Koizumi's spell.

* * *

On February 13, 2007, **Shizuka Kamei**, head of the **Peoples' New Party** and one of Japan's most prominent politicians, spoke at a Budget Committee meeting in the lower house of the Diet. "I can hear a collective groan coming from the farthest reaches of our island nation," he said as he delivered a devastating speech that thoroughly questioned Koizumi's political choices. This was an amazing occasion that overwhelmed the whole roomful of people attending the Budget Committee meeting. He spoke eloquently and with much emotion about how the people of Japan were being neglected.

"We Japanese didn't always have a capitalist economy. We managed with our way of life for thousands of years—is there a reason to drastically Americanize all this right now? The Japanese people should have their own distinct way of living," Kamei said, adding, "Prime minister, I believe this is a truly serious situation. What way of life will lead to happiness for the Japanese people? I would like you to make this the starting point for your economic and social policies."

He blasted Koizumi's policies and insisted that the country needed a politics that was "of the Japanese, by the Japanese and for the Japanese." I believe it was a truly historic speech that laid out a proper path for Japanese politics.

At one point in the speech, Kamei turned to Prime Minister Abe and addressed him directly. "Let us quickly say farewell to Koizumi's policies ... Won't you please run the government based on your own ideas, creed and character? The people won't be angered by this; in fact, everyone would be pleased."

But his plea went unheeded by Abe, who would soon step down in disgrace.

* * *

Just a couple of days before Kamei's historic speech, in the February 11, 2007, edition of the *Tokyo Shimbun*, a widely read daily newspaper, **Koichi Kato**, the former secretary-general of the **Liberal Democratic Party** and still an LDP lawmaker in the lower house, made some comments about the direction Abe seemed to be headed. The article had the following headline: "Kato Says LDP Bound to Lose if It Runs on Constitutional Revision in Upper House Vote; Party Needs to Address Wealth Gap."

At the time, Abe was pushing constitutional revisions to let Japan build its military might. The article reported:

Koichi Kato attended a party for LDP members of the House of Representatives in Tokushima on February 10 and offered some candid advice on Prime Minister Shinzo Abe's plans to focus on constitutional revisions in the House of Councillors election. "If the party is afraid to discuss lifestyle issues, and it focuses on themes like constitutional revision or the right to collective self-defense, it is going to lose badly," he said. "But if it talks in a dignified manner with the opposition **Democratic Party of Japan** about the wealth gap controversy and education problems, the party will see its way to victory."

Kato went on to say that the prime minister's **"rechallenge society,"** which aims to give people a second chance at finding jobs, is at odds with his other catchphrase, "a beautiful nation."

"Japan's beauty comes out when it stresses sympathy and supports its local communities," Kato said, adding that he sees an inherent contradiction between "rechallenge" and "a beautiful nation."

By that time, Abe had become one of those chattering robots spewing forth meaningless platitudes: "a beautiful nation," "set sail from the postwar regime," "constitutional revision," "educational reform." Kato's criticism of the "rechallenge" slogan hit the nail on the head. And of course, history proved him right on the July upper house election, which the LDP lost badly.

Let me repeat this message: the highest priority to be debated right now in Japanese politics should be how to rebuild a Japan so seriously damaged by the Koizumi Revolution. New policies need to be introduced and quickly executed.

Just a few months before Kato and Kamei spoke, the American voters handed George W. Bush's Republican Party a defeat in the midterm elections. The Americans very clearly repudiated Bush's agenda. Bush was able to increase troops to Iraq by about 200,000, but this was his last battle. There is hardly anyone out there who thinks the surge will bring about peace in the streets of Iraq.

The world is about to turn away from war and toward peace. We are moving toward an age where peace will be the goal. At this point in history, any talk of revising **Japan's Constitution** so that Japan's military can coordinate more closely with the US military goes against this global trend and is the height of foolishness.

CHAPTER 3

THE POSTWAR CHOICE
WHAT COUL

DURING HIS SHORT TERM IN OFFICE, FORMER PRIME Minister Abe showed far more interest in the right-wing ideology that has guided Japanese politics during the postwar period than in the minutiae of his predecessor Koizumi's structural reforms. Abe was consciously following in the footsteps of former Prime Minister **Nobusuke Kishi,** his grandfather.

Some people want to deify Kishi. They try to argue that the proper current of Japanese political thought flows from Kishi to **Yasuhiro Nakasone** and onto Koizumi and Abe, but they are completely mistaken. It's a deplorable fallacy that's been perpetuated over the years.

The postwar prime ministers serving under the new Constitution began with Tetsu Katayama and continued through the 50s, 60s, 70s and into the 80s with the following men: Hitoshi Ashida, Shigeru

Yoshida, Ichiro Hatoyama, Tanzan Ishibashi, Kishi, Hayato Ikeda, Eisaku Sato, Kakuei Tanaka, Takeo Miki, Takeo Fukuda, Masayoshi Ohira, Zenko Suzuki and Nakasone.

Ichiro Hatoyama thought seriously about Japan's independence and believed the Constitution needed to be amended to make it easier to escape the American grasp. The first step toward Japan's independence was to establish ties with the Soviet Union, then a

HAVE BEEN

standing member of the United Nations Security Council, and so Hatoyama made Japan a member of the UN.

In those days, Taiwan was still under China's control. The only country that didn't recognize Japan's bid for UN membership was the Soviet Union. Hatoyama re-established ties with the USSR and made Japan's UN membership a reality, returning Japan to the international community. Hatoyama's ultimate goal was independence for Japan.

After Hatoyama came **Tanzan Ishibashi**, who looked to revive relations with the rest of Asia, especially China. But Ishibashi quickly became ill and his cabinet only lasted two months. Ishibashi had said even before World War II that Japan had to survive as part of Asia, but the quick failure of his administration made that goal seem even further away.

When looking at Japan's postwar history, it must be said that Ishibashi's illness was a great loss for the Japanese people. I believe that if Ishibashi had been able to remain as prime minister for an extended period, Japan would have mended fences with the rest of Asia and become part of the region.

The next prime minister, Kishi, was a class-A war criminal who had done time in Sugamo Prison. He was arrested by American General Douglas MacArthur, the supreme commander of the Allied powers, soon after Japan's surrender in 1945. But the US had a conversion of sorts and decided to free Kishi and return him to the political sphere.

Kishi returned to politics in 1953 and became the deputy prime minister and foreign minister in Ishibashi's cabinet. When Ishibashi resigned because of illness, Kishi was deemed his successor and became prime minister in 1957.

When Kishi became the premier, he quickly turned Japan's focus from Asia to the US.

Another defeated country—Germany—had split into east and west halves. West Germany chose to fold itself into Europe once again, finding a way to join hands with its longtime enemy, France. With France and Germany providing a center for Europe, the region was able to overcome many obstacles and ultimately develop into the European Union.

Another Axis power, Italy, also returned to Europe and helped in its rebuilding. Both Germany and Italy chose the path that would free them from US control. Japan should have done the same thing. If it could have forged peace and a stable relationship with China, it could have returned to Asia and not be ruled by the US.

This was Ishibashi's will, but his health failed him and shortened his administration. The dream was effectively crushed as Kishi rose to power.

The Treaty of Perpetual Subordination

Prime Minister **Shigeru Yoshida** did what he could to weaken the American grip on Japan. In those postwar days, the idea of an independent Japan hadn't really sunk in, but he made an effort to resist the American effort to colonize the country. Hatoyama and Ishibashi followed, and they both looked for ways to free Japan from American support, but when Ishibashi fell ill, their goal drifted away. Kishi stepped in and promoted the **Treaty of Mutual Cooperation and Security** between Japan and the US.

In 1952, the **San Francisco Peace Treaty**, which made peace between Japan and the US-led Allied powers, provided peace only in part. Around this time, then Prime Minister Yoshida was all but forced to sign the original **Security Treaty of 1951**. This was a defective treaty without a time limit. The international standard for these sorts of one-way treaties signed by an occupied country is that the treaty is void once the occupation is over. Japan should've worked toward annulling the treaty. Instead, Kishi moved the country toward a new security pact, one that was eventually signed in 1960. Forty-eight years later, this treaty has morphed into the basis for Japan's semipermanent dependence on the US. The Treaty of Mutual Cooperation between Japan and the US has become the Treaty of Perpetual Subordination for Japan.

Lately, debate on this topic has trailed off. Or to put it more precisely, journalists have run from the topic. But if we don't deal with this basic problem, the Japan-US relationship will not change.

Japan could have followed a path similar to the ones traveled by Germany and Italy after World War II. But when Japan was given the choice of putting some distance between itself and the US or in subordinating itself to the US, it unfortunately selected the latter option. Since the Nakasone administration of 1982, every administration, with the sole exception of the **Morihiro Hosokawa** administration, has been a captive of the Americans.

Journalists and politicians continue to hide the basic fact that Japan is a dependent of the US. Japan is a subordinate, yet it acts like an independent country. They trumpet the idea that this subordinate relationship between Japan and the US helps Japan realize more profits. The lies just continue to roll from their tongues.

* * *

Right after the war, during Prime Minister Yoshida's administrations (1946–47, 1948–54), the mass media pretty much as one promoted an anti-war line. In fact, until **Eisaku Sato**'s administration (1964–72), the media took a hard line against any display of administrative strength.

However, by the time Nakasone took the reigns (1982–87), the national newspapers and TV broadcasters had become the allies of national powerbrokers, supporting the Nakasone administration across the board. Japan's media had made a complete reversal.

Japan's newspapers and TV broadcasters use a **press club system**, which makes them reliant on the government. The newspapers and broadcasters are also tied together by the same sources of capital. Because of all this, the media becomes little more than a PR department for the government.

Once the newspapers and broadcasters have teamed up with the government, they only dole out the news that suits their interests. This allows the government's power to grow, while the people become more and more brainwashed.

A democracy begins to take root when all sorts of values are recognized. For democratic politics to flourish, state power must be dispersed. A democratic government comes to the fore when citizens have the power to bring about political change at the voting booth. But today, when media conglomerates work hand in hand with the government, citizens aren't shown a lot of varied information or values. It's like the prewar days have returned and we live under a new Imperial

Rule Assistance Association (a government-initiated national patriotic association that existed in the 1940s). It's a deplorable situation.

Japan is in a period of declining economic power. Just when the country needs to do something, however, it is caught in the grasp of the Bush administration. It has lost its sense of independence. Japan's future is in danger if it doesn't change course. If Japan doesn't do something, it will be pushed into a situation where it will be used up and discarded by the United States.

The recurring nightmare I have when I think about Japan's future is that it is turned into a larger version of Saipan.

Saipan was under German rule until World War I. During the war, Japan took control of the island. It was officially controlled by the League of Nations, but in reality, Japan ran the show. In World War II, the island became a battlefield. After Japan's defeat, the island became the holding of the US military, and in 1947 the United Nations recognized it as a US territory.

For a time, the US showed interest in Saipan. It gave citizens the right to vote and put the island under American rule. But Saipan's citizens never did receive the same rights as other Americans. Once Saipan was under American rule, the Americans soon lost interest in it. Saipan was no longer necessary, another country discarded like a dirty rag.

Won't Japan turn out the same way? We'll be wrung for every last yen we can produce, then flung to the side like a worthless rag. I believe this is what America has in store for us, and it worries me to no end.

To stop Japan from becoming another Saipan, we have to stand together. And Japan has to open its eyes. Japan needs to bring itself up to world standards on a political and cultural level. To do this, the people of Japan need access to all sorts of information and to discuss things from a point of view that accepts all sorts of values. We need to get rid of our uniformity. Japan must pull itself from its destructive relationship with the US and begin to search for its proper path.

CHAPTER 4

LIFE AF

I N MY PREVIOUS BOOK, *AMERICA NI KUI TSUKUSARERU Nippon* (*A Japan Served up for American Consumption*, Nihon Bungeisha, 2006), I interviewed critic Takahiko Soejima. He predicted that the US will use the Finance Ministry to pressure the current administration into raising Japan's consumption tax to 10–15%. We must be prepared for this possibility.

The Koizumi government caved under US pressure and passed the resolution to privatize the postal system. The Americans' next target was Japan's social insurance system. The social insurance coffers are estimated at ¥150–200 trillion. The US is eyeing these funds and has begun making various overtures to get its hands on that money. The Bush administration had prompted the former Koizumi administration to push through reform of the medical system. Could America's goal be to control Japan's health insurance? Then in the final scenario, the US will dip its hands into Japan's tax system. The US government will push for a dramatic increase in Japan's consumption tax, then suck up all the funds.

The Finance Ministry has been mobilizing the media to propagate its campaign of lies about the financial system. The ministry has been trying to convince the Japanese public that the country's

R BUSH

financial system is facing imminent collapse and that the only way out is to dramatically raise the consumption tax. But no matter how hard the ministry tries to trick the public, it won't be that easy. The government that raises the consumption tax will crumble. For politicians of the ruling party, political power is everything; they certainly don't want to lose that.

The Koizumi administration, eager to stay in power, kept putting off the consumption tax issue. Any hike in the tax would further slow already stagnant consumer spending. A forced consumption-tax increase potentially raises the specter of a third consumer crisis, following the ones triggered by the Takeshita and Hashimoto cabinets. A panic will dramatically slow the economy, pushing the country's GDP into negative territory.

A consumption tax increase during these slow times would only crush the Japanese economy and drag down the leadership that initiated it. That's why Koizumi evaded the issue all along.

America is at war right now. A considerable amount of that war is being funded by Japan. The cost of keeping US bases in Japan notwithstanding, our nation is also expected to shoulder the cost of transferring troops as part of an American military reorganization. The Japanese government is about to spend as much as six billion dollars to build homes for the US military on Guam.

Huge amounts of money are required to continue fighting in Iraq and Afghanistan. The US wants Japan to foot the bill. It also wants Japan to take care of future US military spending. We mustn't be surprised therefore that the US may be eyeing Japan's consumption tax as a source of funding.

Democrats Won't Help Japan Much

I predict that a Democrat will be elected this fall as the next US president. What will happen to Japanese politics then? In between the Reagan (1981–1989) and Bush administrations' (2001–) Republican reign was eight years of Democratic rule under the Clinton administration from 1993. During the Clinton era, President Bill Clinton and then Prime Minister **Kiichi Miyazawa** exchanged the first annual **US-Japan Regulatory Reform and Competition Policy Initiative**. Under the initiative set forth by the US, Japan proceeded with its reforms, began to privatize its postal service and established a system that would make available to the US ¥350 trillion in Japan's postal funds.

In other words, the changing of the guard from Republican to Democratic rule will not alter the American government's goal of sucking wealth out of Japan.

However, upon closer inspection of the American government's policies toward Japan, there is a clear difference between the Republican and Democratic parties.

Under the Bush administration, Japan helped fund the Iraq War and dispatched its Self-Defense Forces, ostensibly for reconstruction assistance. Japan was used by the Bush administration in war and for its economy. But under a Democratic leadership, the war cry will ease a bit, eventually leading to US withdrawal from Iraq. By how much will the war tab decrease? It's hard to say, but the fundamental goal of sucking wealth out of Japan won't change.

The sad part is that Japan can become free only after it has been all used up and tossed out by the US. Japan is indeed heading down a tragic path. Only firm political will can stop this.

CHAPTER 5

ANTAGONIZING CHINA THE FAVORITE SPORT

*Morality prevails
where absolute power fails.*

— KOBUN SHINPO

THOSE WHO RELY ON ABSOLUTE POWER TO REGULATE society always fail. Those who walk the moral or ethical path become the kings of the world. This is the law of nature.

The first part of this saying—that those who rely on absolute power will ultimately fail — is a kind of historical law. US President Bush has about a half year left in his term. Former Prime Minister Koizumi, Bush's lap dog, was able to avoid a sordid fate as he finished his term, but he is the exception to the rule. It's as if he were smart enough to know when to run away. This is because of the stupidity of Japan's mass media, which saved Koizumi by practically turning him into a saint.

But that's not to say that Koizumi will live in peace from now on. That would be virtually impossible. People who commit crimes must be punished. The Japanese people will realize soon that the many ills afflicting their society have their roots in Koizumi's politics. Many people are already starting to realize this.

In former Prime Minister Abe's book, *Abe Shinzo Taironshuu* (*The Collected Theories of Shinzo Abe*), he writes the following in a chapter entitled "Assessing Japan's Diplomatic Situation": "When dealing with North Korea, it is vital that we take a very strong stance."

We can explain Abe's political views this way: "Excluding the US and all of its allies, we should take a very strong stance toward other countries, especially if the US hates them." It will be difficult for the

JAPAN'S NEOCONS

rest of the world to take seriously this sort of schoolyard bully approach to diplomacy.

By following Abe's strong-arm approach to dealing with the world, Japan will be viewed as nothing more than America's lesser partner, as being essentially part of America. Japan's government would be the "mini-America government." I am not being flippant: this result is very possible.

The Japanese people can't let this happen. We should be far more afraid than we are of the power we gave the Liberal Democratic Party and **New Komeito**, which together still hold two-thirds of the lower-house seats. It's time to stand up to this sort of thinking.

The thinking of people such as Abe in Japan is very similar to the thinking of the neoconservatives in the US: take over the government, grab control of the media and brainwash the citizens, then put the military in action against Islamic countries. In Abe's world view, there is no place for peace or harmony, only strong-arm politics.

Over the last four years in the US, the neocons have lost the support of the American people because of Bush's war. The Americans have awoken from their brainwashing and started to look with anger at their president. Bush's Republicans went down to defeat in the November 2006 midterm elections. The US is beginning to distance itself from the Bush legacy.

Koizumi and Abe, both hardcore right-wingers, are the Japanese version of neocons. The Japanese electorate showed in July 2007 that it, too, was waking up to the truth about its political leaders when it overwhelmingly defeated the LDP and New Komeito in a House of Councillors election, handing the opposition control of the upper house for the first time in sixty years.

When Koizumi's Supporters Realize Everything Has Gone Wrong

While Japan's neocons talk loudly about the dangers of China, a much larger danger—in fact, China doesn't even compare—can be found in Bush's America. I believe we should be deeply suspicious of attempts to colonize Japan and exhaust Japanese assets.

What the Bush government is doing to Japan is atrocious.

It used Koizumi to push through privatization of Japan's postal system, freeing up ¥340 trillion in assets. The Japanese people watched as the money they had toiled to make and then saved over a lifetime in postal savings and life-insurance accounts was turned over to the international markets. Instead of having the Japanese government monitor the funds, now traders were making the decisions—all in the name of that harmless little buzzword, "privatization."

When a public corporation turns private, in essence, the people with the most stock become the managers. The strong American funds will win. American corporations in general are still far more powerful than Japanese corporations. Sooner or later, an American firm will come in and control a postal-related corporation in Japan. The chances of this happening are quite high.

The day when former Koizumi supporters look around and say, "It wasn't supposed to be like this" is not that far away, I think.

The American government came up with the idea of realigning US troops in Japan, and yet it wants Japan to foot the bill. A US Defense Department official said that Japan owed three trillion yen for the realignment, but this is not something Japan should bear. In fact, it shouldn't pay a single yen. Of course, none of the elite in the Koizumi cabinet could bring themselves to say no.

The conversation came to a point where a payment of "about two trillion yen" was bandied about, but this is just ridiculous. Can we really say that Japan is a sovereign nation with this kind of talk?

Former Diet member **Kouki Kobayashi** writes that Japan has become "the greatest contributor to the US."

During Abe's term as prime minister, it was easy to say that he just didn't have a clue. But that's not true. He understood exactly what was going on, and that's why he raised his voice to complain about China.

The main reason for Japan's drifting about in the modern world is its subordination to the US. Japan's decline has nothing to do with China. Japan is declining because of the US. But Abe never touched on the issue of Japan's subordination to the US. He just kept emphasizing that "the US-Japan relationship is connected by a strong sense of mutual trust." That's quite a cloud of obfuscation from the former premier.

* * *

"To renounce liberty is to renounce being a man, to surrender the rights of humanity and even its duties. For him who renounces everything, no indemnity is possible."
— JEAN JACQUES ROUSSEAU

I'd like to try to interpret Rousseau's words in a slightly different way: "To renounce independence is to renounce being a nation. For a nation that abandons everything, becoming a slave state is all that is left."

Returning to Abe's *Collected Theories* for a moment, the people involved in this book are a who's who of Japanese neoconservatism. In chapter ten, Abe is interviewed by **Yoshihisa Komori**, editor-at-large in Washington DC for the ***Sankei Shimbun***. Komori is a neocon journalist who completely defends the American government and the government in Taiwan. He's a journalist of the "Taiwan tribe." His hatred of China is unusually pronounced. He is the poster boy for the anti-China journalist camp.

Turn the page to chapter eleven, and Professor **Terumasa Nakanishi** of Kyoto University appears. In chapter thirteen, **Yoshiko Sakurai** interviews Abe and makes her fourth appearance in the book. Add **Yoshiyuki Kasai** and **Hidetsugu Yagi**, and you have the stars of Japan's neocon galaxy.

Abe and this bunch believe the following: 1) they adore the US-Japan alliance and Bush's neocon politics; 2) they worship Koizumi; 3) they want to model Japan after Anglo-Saxon societies; 4) they viscerally dislike China; 5) they hold the rest of Asia in contempt; 6) they see no reason to apologize for Japanese actions during World War II; 7) they're not afraid of starting a war. Read carefully what these people write, and these views will inevitably ooze out.

The North Korean Nuclear Missile Myth

Professor Nakanishi wrote *Shin Nichu Senso Wa Mou Hajimatteiru* (*The New War between Japan and China Has Already Started*, Bungei Shunju 2006). As a neocon, Nakanishi aligns himself with the American neocons in trying to get Japan and China to confront each other by stirring up a dispute. He's a provocateur trying to fan the flames of war between Japan and China.

The American government has succeeded in provoking and opposing North Korea and using that tension to make the Japanese people think that their security is threatened and that if they don't run to the US for help, they'll be the target of a North Korean nuclear missile attack. They need to listen to the US, the conventional wisdom goes, and pay whatever the US requests to remain safe. The neocons have pulled this off quite successfully.

The Americans have very skillfully used North Korea to keep Japan under control, but this era has come to a close. Many Japanese citizens have awoken to the fact that they've been adeptly manipulated by the Americans on this issue.

Of course, there are not many Japanese who have shaken off the effects of their brainwashing. Moreover, some Japanese have already lost that sense of being a citizen of an independent country—that sense that we are ultimately the ones who must defend our country. Is there another country in the world as big as Japan—127 million people—that has lost this sense of being ready to defend itself? Political leaders, bureaucrats, financiers, the mass media and many of Japan's citizens have grown accustomed to relying on the US. We should be very concerned.

Abe, Nakanishi and the other Japanese neocons see this sort of saber-rattling with North Korea and get all excited. "The Japanese sense of pride in their country is on the rise!" Have they completely lost their minds?

This idea that the North Koreans have the intention and the capability to launch a nuclear attack on Japan is not something that the Japanese government has investigated or concluded on its own. The Japanese government received a leak from the US government and fed it to the Japanese press, which spread the rumors far and wide.

This is the way the US does things:

First a high-ranking US official will visit North Korea and talk with Kim Jong-il. Before the US official returns to Washington, he or she makes a stop in Tokyo. The official will tell officials in the Japanese government that a well-placed source in the North Korean leadership said the country has nuclear missiles ready to attack Tokyo. The Japanese officials hear this and go to the domestic press. Then the media reports as if the nuclear missiles are practically on their way. The Japanese people then feel that they need to turn to the Americans, who are the only ones with the power to get rid of those missiles.

In other words, through the manipulations of government leaders in both the US and Japan, the Japanese sense of pride in their nation collapses. If the US strikes fear in the hearts of the Japanese over a potential North Korean attack, then they have succeeded in reducing Japan to a US dependent.

Japan unconditionally surrendered to the Americans at the end of World War II and took its place under US management. After achieving independence with the San Francisco Peace Treaty, two subsequent security treaties left Japan in a semipermanent state of subordination to the US.

One year after the attacks in the US on 9/11, the North Korean nuclear missile issue arose to spoil any sense of independence the Japanese may have had. The Japanese government and the media worked together with the US government to destroy Japan's independent spirit.

The Japanese people are about to wake up. They've been in a hypnotic state thanks to the efforts of the Bush administration, the governments of Koizumi, Abe and **Yasuo Fukuda**, the coalition partner New Komeito, the Buddhist lay organization **Soka Gakkai** and the advertising giant **Dentsu**. The independent spirit—the spirit of an independent nation—will rise again in the Japanese people.

For the US, tension between Japan and China is not a bad thing. I suppose that deep down, the US wishes for some sort of strife to break out between the two Asian nations. The US-Japan alliance is strengthened as tensions between Japan and China rise. If the Asian region becomes unstable, American influence rises. It's an illusion to equate the US-Japan alliance with Asian stability as long as America continues on its imperialist path.

In other words, the US-Japan alliance is a threat to both Asian and global stability. With Bush at the helm, the very existence of the US poses a threat to regional and world peace. Look at the world today and there is no bigger threat than the imperial ambitions of the Bush administration. At home, Koizumi and Abe have been Bush's junior partners.

We need to renew and reconfirm our priorities for the world. We cherish peace. We don't make war. Waging war is the worst possible outcome. War is the one thing we must end.

CHAPTER 6

THE WAR ON

The Trinity Reforms, first introduced in 2003 by then Prime Minister Koizumi and the Council of Economic and Fiscal Policy, have been debated ever since. Essentially, the plan calls for decentralization of taxes, meaning that the national government will give fewer subsidies to local governments, transfer some tax authority to them and review its grants. Proponents of the plan say it's a way for local governments to stand on their own two feet, but Mr. Morita explains that something far more sinister is at hand.

I BELIEVE THAT ONE PART OF KOIZUMI'S SO-CALLED TRINITY Reforms — the part that calls for a realignment of Japanese provinces into large states — is ultimately a policy meant to render the provinces powerless.

Koizumi was fond of saying that the Trinity Reforms would "increase the independence of local governments, foster familiarity with citizens and make way for policies that suit the different aspects of each region." This is why, the former premier would say, "we must re-examine the roles of the nation and the provinces, make public financing more independent and aim to establish autonomous regions through decentralization of the provinces."

IE PROVINCES

But it is now very clear that he was speaking in meaningless platitudes. The Trinity Reforms are speeding up the destruction of the provinces. The truth behind the so-called decentralization of the provinces is that these outlying areas are unable to develop.

The plan to make Japan into states would have smaller areas and prefectures merging together to create larger regions ruled by a local government. There is one plan under consideration that would put all the authority in these super-provinces with the exception of diplomacy and military affairs.

At a meeting of the National Governors' Association, the Trinity Reforms were billed as a "step on the way to a truly decentralized society by reforming and reviving public financing." But the actual position of the people who have put this policy forth remains unclear.

What is clear is that the government officials and politicians who came up with this plan are intent on doing away with smaller municipalities and eventually prefectures. Many politicians in both the Liberal Democratic Party and the opposition Democratic Party of Japan talk about changing over to a state system, but their talk never proceeds beyond abstractions. If they really understood Japan's provinces, they'd realize that they need to start working toward the revitalization of the cities, towns and villages. Without them, Japan's rural society will be lost. We need knowledge and money to revive these rural hubs. Japan seems to have lost touch with its roots. This talk about forming states always starts with people saying they want to strengthen the provinces, but eventually it becomes the trump card for doing the provinces in. This is where the danger lies in these abstract talks on the united states of Japan.

Japan's Orwellian Double-Speak

LDP Secretary-General **Hidenao Nakagawa** likes to advocate a "rising tide lifts all boats" philosophy when it comes to economics. His views boil down to "if Tokyo thrives, so do the provinces; if big companies grow, so will the small ones." But the leaders of the largest corporations care only about their own bottom lines. The leaders of Japan's largest corporations are all so full of themselves, there's no room for anyone else. They don't think at all about Japan's smaller companies. If big companies are profitable—and if they personally are profitable—they're satisfied. Tokyo Governor **Shintaro Ishihara** is cut from the same cloth: If Tokyo prospers, that's all he cares about. He's the sort who cares only about his own cut.

The governor of a certain prefecture recently lamented to me: "As we get into the lobbying season, I have to make several trips to Tokyo." Subsidies have gotten smaller, and the competition for them is stiff. A governor who makes the rounds in Tokyo ten times during the season is likely to land more money for his prefecture than a governor who only visits five times. So if the governor of the neighboring prefecture is going ten times, you have to go too. And you have to stay overnight in Tokyo. If you stay at a hotel that costs ten thousand yen a night, then you're giving two hundred yen to Tokyo in the form of a hotel tax.

"For us to appeal for funds, we have to go to Tokyo, do our lobbying and watch Tokyo get fat," moaned the governor. "It makes me so mad."

The system works to fatten Tokyo and Tokyo alone.

While everybody talks about "decentralization," the truth is that power is more centralized than before. The government talks about reducing subsidies to give the local governments more autonomy, but that's the opposite of what is actually happening. The reduced subsidies are setting off intense competition among the provinces.

I repeat: the government is using the issue of statehood to abandon the cities, towns and villages in the provinces. And that's not all. The next step is to get rid of the prefectures. Across the board, the government turns the term "decentralization" on its head. It has also twisted the meaning of "economic revival." The state of an economy used to be gauged by how well the citizens were doing. Now the government couldn't care less about the citizens—if the major corporations are profiting, then everything's fine. A good economy is now one where large corporations have equally large profits.

This is how the government turns language on its head.

Abandoned

From a May 2003 interview of Minoru Morita by Takehiko Kambayashi

Kambayashi: You see a lot of Japan as you give lectures throughout the country. Can you tell us what you see outside Tokyo these days?

Morita: In the provinces, the economic situation has become much more serious. The only prosperous place in Japan right now is Tokyo.

Many people say that there are now two Japans — Tokyo, in a bubble, and the provinces, in a deep recession.

K: When you say "Tokyo in a bubble," what do you mean?

M: Tokyo is isolated and insulated from the rest of the country. This is primarily a result of the policies of the Koizumi cabinet. It has drastically tightened its fiscal control over the provinces. The administration makes it clear that it will stick to its policy of fiscal restraint, so local governments are being forced to merge with each other. They simply cannot operate under such policies.

Second, during the period of rapid economic expansion, the provinces followed Tokyo as a model. Main streets named Ginza are everywhere. But the protracted economic downturn has hit the provinces hard. Many stores along Main Street are shuttered now.

Leading companies are abandoning the provinces and converging on Tokyo because there are more business opportunities in the capital. This abandonment is happening even in big cities like Nagoya and Osaka. It is only in Tokyo that you can make good money. So whenever leaders of Osaka-based Matsushita Electric go to meetings, they are pressured by people who say things like, "It seems like Matsushita is the only corporation that is not going to Tokyo. Why?" The provinces are being hollowed out.

When I was invited to Kagoshima a year ago, the city seemed deserted. I said to my hosts, "Where are all the people?" They told me there is only one place where people gather, and they took me to that place. It was a local employment agency. Wherever you go outside Tokyo, you notice the same thing: the only place where many people meet is the local employment agency. The number of jobless keeps increasing outside of Tokyo; they say the jobless rates outside of the capital are higher than the national average by 2–3%.

As local economies deteriorate, even the yakuza and taxi drivers are coming to Tokyo. Tokyo draws those looking to prosper. On the other hand, while the provinces have lost prosperity, morality has resurged. Thus Japan has polarized: The provinces are poor but regaining their sense of morality, and Tokyo is prosperous but morally adrift, focused completely on making money, and thus attracting more crime.

K: It seems that more politicians, scholars and journalists are writing off egalitarianism these days.

M: Yes. The Koizumi cabinet has made significant progress in polarizing society: the rich and the poor; the prosperous megalopolis and the struggling provinces. They have destroyed our egalitarian society. The government's policies are based on the idea that Japan has been unable to realize its potential even though the Japanese people are naturally more able than others. In the late 1970s, an American scholar, Ezra Vogel, mockingly flattered Japan in a book called *Japan as Number One*. Many Japanese, including top scholars, took this seriously and became flushed with Japan's importance.

It's just like a pinch hitter who comes in with the bases loaded, closes his eyes, swings and happens to hit a grand slam. The Japanese mistook dumb luck for true ability. Japanese bureaucrats continue in this misconception.

In short, what the administration is trying to do is turn Japan into Toyota. It is trying to make the rest of Japan follow the example of its only successful business model. In order to do this, the government makes no bones about slashing workers' wages and welfare and creating more unemployment. As you know, it's absolutely impossible for all of Japan to become Toyota. When I visited Toyota City in Aichi Prefecture the other day, locals told me that while Toyota Motors has flourished, Toyota City has not.

K: Many people say Japan should decentralize. Do you see decentralization happening in the provinces?

M: The "decentralization" the government promotes is false. It is reinforcing centralization under the slogan of "decentralization." The government tells the provinces to follow "decentralization plans" made by the central government. Major newspapers and networks accept these plans at face value, but in the provinces, they are seen as centralization. It is sad but true that the majority of the public also misconstrues these plans as decentralization. However, a minority believes that the provinces need to achieve a true decentralization of power—and these people say the first step should be to start turning their back on the national government.

For the record: City officials say then mayor Kohei Suzuki met with Minoru Morita after Morita had made a speech in the city. They confirmed that the mayor told Morita Toyota City hasn't thrived in the way Toyota Motors has, but they also stressed that city residents have not been having a hard time making ends meet. They say the Toyota group has contributed to the region's economic well-being.

A Company Town

*Yoshinori Omura, a **Communist Party** member who was serving his third term as city councillor in Toyota City, talked with Takehiko Kambayashi in early 2008.*

Toyota City has forty-seven city councillors. Ten out of the forty-seven are endorsed by Toyota Motors or Toyota group labor unions. They are effectively members of the Democratic Party of Japan, though officially they are independents.

The city had had no Communist Party members on the council for years when I first won the election ten years ago. It was unthinkable. Typcially in Japan, if you have forty or fifty city councillors, you have at least four or five Communist Party members. It was almost impossible for our party members even to run for an election here since the Toyota group has so much influence on city politics. I used to live in Hekinan City, next to Toyota City. I moved to Toyota to run for the election. Another party member won an election last year. That makes just two council members from the Communist Party.

Toyota has layers of subcontractors and they also own some companies that are not related to the carmaking business. Put all these together and Toyota has about four thousand subcontractors and business establishments. About 70% of them are family-run businesses or small factories. The small factories are making car parts for Toyota. Without them, Toyota would not exist. The problem is that only 30% of those small factories and family-run businesses have been able to turn a profit in recent years. The rest, 70% of them, are losing money. You may wonder why they are able to continue doing business if they're losing money. That is because they continue to get orders from Toyota even as their profit margins shrink due to pressure from Toyota or other companies in the group. Small factories have to obey their demand. Imagine the shrinking profit margin that small enterprises at the bottom of the group can get.

Some people take it for granted that Toyota employees are getting good salaries. The fact is most of them don't. Their base pay is very low. But they also get overtime pay, night-shift allowances and other types of payments.

Their base pay is so low that the average worker's retirement allowance is around twelve million yen (about $120,000) even after working at the company for thirty years. Is that the kind of reward an employee at the world's best company should get?

Labor Thanksgiving Day is celebrated on November 23 in Japan, but Toyota employees have to work. They have another calendar called a Toyota calendar that they use because of production schedules.

Employees also work overtime without pay. Recently one ex-worker's wife filed a lawsuit against Toyota, alleging that her husband's death was due to overwork, or *karoshi*, because he logged so much overtime work at the Toyota plant. Her husband collapsed inside the factory at dawn one day. The company said he was chatting with his coworkers, but she claimed he was discussing quality control with them. She won the lawsuit.

Labor exploitation is rampant inside the Toyota group. Without it, they could not have surpassed GM. While Toyota has prospered, its employees are poor. I don't think its employees are treated as human beings. One of the most serious problems in Japan now is the widening gap between the rich and poor. I can see the epitome of it in Toyota City and the Toyota group.

Toyota employees are not really getting a fair share of Toyota's prosperity. Toyota citizens also struggle with the economic downturn. We have seen big department stores in the city such as Sogo, Nagasakiya and SATY closing down over these past ten years. Since Sogo left, the big building in front of the station has been empty. Construction of the building was supported by the city. That means the project was helped by taxpayers. Finally, Matsuzakaya department store moved in.

Toyota affiliates, however small they are, have in-house organizations. These organizations gather information on employees and their family members and try to control their voting behavior. They try to prevent them from voting freely.

CHAPTER 7

THE BATTLE F(

Mr. Morita wrote passionately on a contentious mayoral election in Iwakuni City in February 2008. The election centered on a plan by the national government to relocate several carrier-borne aircraft of the US military to Iwakuni and expand an already existing US military base. The city's mayor rose up in opposition to the plan and rallied voters to stand up to the government plan. He officially resigned his post to hold an election against a pro-realignment candidate and seek a mandate for his views. But then the campaign turned dirty, with the national government withholding promised subsidies unless the mayoral candidates agreed to the **US military realignment plan.** *Rumors spread about the city's dismal future if the incumbent candidate should prevail. Veiled threats were made. Morita became part of the election by making frequent trips on behalf of the incumbent.*

We share four of his columns from his website — three before and one after the election — along with original reporting by Takehiko Kambayashi, a Japan correspondent for papers including the Christian Science Monitor *and* The Washington Times. *Kambayashi interviewed voters in the area to give us a firsthand picture of an already forgotten but important local election.*

IWAKUNI CITY

» **Minoru Morita Unravels Japan**
» January 23, 2008
» DETAINED BY POLICE
» *The Yamaguchi prefectural police treated me like a suspect when I walked near US military bases in Iwakuni City*

The US military base in Iwakuni City is of a size and scale far beyond anything I had imagined. As the Bush regime winds down and East Asia lives peacefully, what in the world could be the possible justification for a military base of this size? Why do the US and Japanese governments want to enhance the base? The injustice of it all makes me furious.

On the morning of January 13, 2008, I was led by Jungen Tamura, a member of the Iwakuni City Council, on a tour of the area surrounding the US military base in that city. Councilman Tamura was a splendid host. I felt very honored to be with him.

Our tour of the coastal land reserved for expanding the US base was an extraordinary experience. As we stood on a public road looking over the land, a Yamaguchi prefectural patrol car approached us. Two policemen got out. "Who are you?" one of them asked, and we replied, "Tourists."

"From where?"

"Tokyo," I said.

"So what is this?" asked Tamura. "Why are you asking these questions?"

"We question suspicious persons," came the reply. "Do you have a driver's license?"

Our driver gave the policeman his license. The policeman looked it over and returned it.

There were two other guides with Tamura and me. They were local government employees from Hiroshima Prefecture—all of us were well dressed.

"Whenever I approach the US military base, a prefectural patrol car comes," Tamura said. "The US military must be requesting it."

People connected with the US military must be feeling particularly nervous, I thought.

For more than a decade, I have lectured three times a year at the National Police Academy. I believe the police are a necessary part of society, and basically I trust Japanese police officers.

I had never thought that just by passing US military land on a sightseeing excursion, I could be thought of as a suspicious person. I think this incident reveals the truth that Iwakuni City belongs to the US military. It also hints at the larger truth that Japan is a servant of the US. This is the underlying truth of the US-Japan relationship. The first duty of the Japanese police is to keep the people of Japan safe. I can't agree with a policy that has people being treated with suspicion just for walking near a US military base.

I went to see the Atagoyama development, which is part of the Iwakuni base expansion plan; the Japanese government and the Yamaguchi prefectural government are planning to turn the area into living quarters for US soldiers. This area was supposed to be home to a typical residential development, but once most of the land had been leveled, that project was cancelled. To prepare for the residential development, the prefectural government bought parcels of land from different landowners, and now the prefecture is conveniently the sole owner of the property in question. The rumor is that the prefecture plans to sell the land to the Defense Ministry. A person researching the issue told me, "The government and the prefecture probably planned all along to use the land to house the American military."

The earth taken from the Atagoyama development was used to reclaim land from the sea and build a new runway. Iwakuni residents have long been bothered by the loud noises of US military planes passing overhead, and this new runway was supposed to ease their burden. But as soon as enough earth was taken from Atagoyama to build the reclaimed runway, the Atagoyama housing project was cancelled.

Now the plan is to sell the land to the Defense Ministry and develop housing for newly transferred US military personnel from bases in Okinawa and Atsugi. Former Vice Defense Minister **Takemasa Moriya**, who has been indicted on corruption charges, was said to be the main force behind the plan.

I have seen the whole project from the outside: the path of the belt conveyors that transported the Atagoyama soil, the US military base, the army post for US military personnel, the lodgings and the rest of it. From my vantage point, I couldn't help but suspect that all along the plan was to develop housing for the US military, that the Atagoyama project was intentionally and systematically planned. I dare say that the residents of Iwakuni City were fed misinformation and tricked into this plan. As I gazed at the vast military base, I was struck by the furtive movements of high-ranking American and Japanese government officials over this Iwakuni property.

I believe there's a need to look into this — that the grand plan to turn Iwakuni into Asia's largest US military base had been in place for about ten years and is being cleverly carried out as I speak.

We must not let the maneuverings of former Vice Defense Minister Moriya and his cohorts extinguish the flames of democracy and autonomy in Iwakuni City. I call for the nation to stand behind former Iwakuni Mayor Ihara as he fights for the city's autonomy.

Incumbent Iwakuni Mayor **Katsusuke Ihara** is a great man. He has admonished the Defense Ministry for its mistakes, and for that, he deserves praise. I feel deep respect for Ihara's hard work for justice.

Meanwhile, former Vice Defense Minister Takemasa Moriya and his supporters have reneged on their promise to the city, unilaterally withdrawing government subsidies, then announcing to Ihara that approval of the US military reorganization plan and the transfer of American carrier-borne aircraft were conditions for reinstating those subsidies. This carrot-and-stick approach is just plain mean.

The American military reorganization plan was a strategy cooked up under war President Bush, former Defense Secretary Donald Rumsfeld and former Deputy Secretary of State Richard Armitage. This strategy will very likely be re-evaluated when Bush steps down. Former Prime Minister Koizumi, successive directors-general of the Defense Ministry (and the former Defense Agency), Moriya and his cohorts — as well as the usual hawkish suspects — were loyal supporters of the Bush military strategy.

Moriya was the central figure behind the plan to expand the US military base in Iwakuni and to transfer the US aircraft carriers from the US military base in Atsugi, Kanagawa Prefecture, to Iwakuni. Moriya supporters are now using aggressive tactics to force through the transfer, trampling all over the wishes of Iwakuni residents, who just want safety and peace of mind.

Ihara is a courageous and intelligent man. He is trying to right the wrongs committed by the American government, the Japanese government, the Defense Ministry and the LDP. A majority of Iwakuni residents support Ihara's political stance.

But as the mayoral election scheduled for February 10 approaches, agents of the Defense Ministry, the LDP and those behind the Iwakuni base agreement have been trying to slice apart the opposition to the base expansion by sending out advertisements with the following message: "It's useless for Iwakuni residents to oppose the plan. You'll be much better off accepting the base expansion plan, having the carrier-borne aircraft transferred from Atsugi and accepting the money from the Defense Ministry." I've seen and read many flyers with this sort of message distributed around Iwakuni City.

But that's not all they say. "Resisting the nation will send Iwakuni City into bankruptcy. It will be like Yubari City all over again," the flyers say, referring to the bankrupt Hokkaido mining town that tried but failed to reinvent itself as a tourist destination when the government refused to help it with its growing debt. The propaganda is being hammered into the city's consciousness. This is the despicable work of henchmen for the Japanese government and the Defense Ministry.

"Emergency medical services and community health care will no longer exist!!" The sense of crisis is fueled by this sort of exaggeration. "Taxes will go up!!" The claims are baseless, yet they are shamelessly propagated.

Then there are the carrots: Overblown ads proclaim that if the military base expansion is allowed to go through, government money will flow into the city. It's malignant. If the LDP is pulling the strings here, then I really have to protest its complete loss of dignity.

Getting a little money in exchange for taking on a US military base is the equivalent of selling your soul. And that's not all. It would effectively be selling off Iwakuni's future. Consider the hardships borne by people living around the US bases in Okinawa and Atsugi. If you think about the difficulties borne by the children and grandchildren of those families—the effects go far into the future—the carrots and sticks being used here by the Defense Ministry and the pro-US military crowd are nothing short of toxic. This cannot be forgiven.

This next column appeared on Morita's website four days before the mayoral election in Iwakuni.

» **Minoru Morita Unravels Japan**
» February 6, 2008
» THE WIND AT OUR BACKS (THE BATTLE FOR IWAKUNI)

More than ten days ago, on January 19, 2008, to be precise, I took part in a large grass-roots movement in support of Iwakuni City's former Mayor Katsusuke Ihara. I received a write-up of the event, which appeared in the *Chugoku Shimbun*, from Yasutake Hayashi, a former city councilman in Shoubara, Hiroshima Prefecture, whom I became acquainted with in Iwakuni. Here's what it said:

> Ihara's supporters held a large grass-roots rally under the banner "Strength to the Wind!" at the local citizen's hall. Speakers included political commentator Minoru Morita and Hatsukaichi City Mayor Saburo Yamashita. There were about 1,700 supporters in attendance, according to organizers.
>
> Ihara spoke in opposition to the proposed relocation of US military facilities and personnel: "The reorganization of the US military is the most important issue here. Depending on which side wins, the results of the military transfer will flip 180 degrees. Even if we get some sort of paltry subsidy for having the base transferred here, only a small group of people will profit," Ihara said.

"Iwakuni is our beacon of hope," Morita said in support of Ihara's stance. "We must protect democracy and local autonomy." Yamashita also cried out, "I want everyone to make an effort for the sake of local autonomy throughout Japan!"

Ihara and Morita spoke together in front of JR Iwakuni Station.

Lately all I've been able to think about is the Iwakuni mayoral election, which is just four days from now. Asleep or awake, I'm constantly worrying about this vote. Will the people of Iwakuni think about their future or grab the money being dangled before their eyes? This election could represent a turning point for the future of Japan.

Between now and February 10, I want to make time to help Ihara in his quest. The choice of Iwakuni's voters—justice or money – will have a large influence on Japan's future path, I believe. We have to work to ensure that justice is victorious.

IWAKUNI MAYORAL ELECTION RESULTS

Yoshihiko Fukuda	47,081
Katsusuke Ihara	45,299

(Voter turnout: 76%)

Voice of the Voters I

Shigeki Yamane is an Iwakuni resident in his mid-thirties.

Former Iwakuni Mayor Ihara's defeat in the hard-fought election disappointed many. Soon after that, however, various citizen movements have surfaced. Despite the loss, one good point is more citizens closely monitor what Mayor Yoshihiko Fukuda is doing. In general, more citizens seem to have become aware of political and social issues. So, I would say we are lucky the results weren't worse.

During the election campaign, a group of women who we called "the band of whisperers" would go around the city and have loud conversations. They'd gather at hospitals, eateries or on the bus and talk a little too loudly about how Iwakuni was going to go bankrupt. They made sure everyone could hear. They were adopting scare tactics, saying, "Iwakuni will follow in the footsteps of Yubari if nothing is done."

We heard a lot of rumors. For example, one such rumor was that the president of a local contractor gave his employees ten thousand yen each if they promised to vote for Fukuda. The contractors were working very hard to get Fukuda elected, taking their employees to the polling place, for example. Many citizens have been struggling since the region's economic situation has deteriorated. Most of them cannot afford to look at the big picture. They were just going after immediate gains. Young parents are supposed to think about creating a safe environment where their child will grow up, but these parents were also coaxed into voting for Fukuda, since they heard child-care and school lunches might be free if Fukuda were elected. The fact that Fukuda has three children was also a good sales point, I think.

I believe Mr. Ihara made a good fight of it even though he was a target of a smear campaign. He got more votes than many had expected. We believe this has only begun.

» **Minoru Morita Unravels Japan**

» February 20, 2008

» JAPAN'S REBIRTH DEPENDS UPON ESCAPING AMERICA

» *The* Shinano Mainichi *newspaper gets it right in reporting on the Iwakuni problem. Are the Americans paying attention?*

F-san, a 50-year-old man who lives in Yokohama, sent me a newspaper article from the February 13 issue of the *Shinano Mainichi* newspaper the other day. He attached the following message: "We've been saved just a little bit by some serious journalism." The article he sent was titled "What the Voters Didn't Understand about the Iwakuni Mayoral Election." Thank you, F-san. I would like to share an excerpt from the article:

> In the latest mayoral election in Iwakuni City, Yamaguchi Prefecture, former Liberal Democratic Party lower house lawmaker Yoshihiko Fukuda, who declared he would relocate US military aircraft to the city, defeated former Mayor Katsusuke Ihara, who opposed the relocation.
>
> To push the relocation, the Japanese government applied pressure through subsidies. It appears that the concerns of local residents about air pollution and other issues were bulldozed aside by national policy. In the end, the vote was very close.
>
> This mayoral "victory" has only served to push into the spotlight the problem of relocating US military aircraft. We ask that the country not force its will on the people but instead engage them in a polite dialogue.
>
> The relocation of aircraft for carriers was included in the autumn 2005 US-Japan governmental agreement on the relocation of US troops. The plan called for transferring fifty-nine aircraft from the Atsugi base in Kanagawa Prefecture.
>
> This election has exposed the Japanese government's blasé attitude toward the country's citizens.
>
> Iwakuni City has twice rejected the relocation. The first time was in a referendum in March 2006. Ninety percent voted against the base relocation.
>
> The second time was in April 2006, as the city was deciding whether to merge with surrounding towns and villages. Former Mayor Ihara, who was against the relocation, won the election in a landslide.

The thing that changed this time was the way the government forced its message on the people. Because Ihara was against the base relocation, the government froze subsidies to help build a new city hall after construction was already under way. The city felt the financial pinch, and relations worsened between the mayor and the city council, which was controlled by a majority in favor of the aircraft relocation. Ihara was faced with no other choice but to resign and run again in search of a mandate.

An exit poll by Kyodo News showed that support for Fukuda was strongest in the old suburban districts that were far from the proposed base. It is likely that in the neighborhoods little affected by the noise pollution of the aircraft, the idea of having an estimated thirteen billion yen in federal subsidies for the region proved the clincher.

The results show how the federal government used carrots and sticks to bring in a new mayor. There is nothing praiseworthy about how it got in the way of the management of a municipality.

The people most affected by the aircraft relocation and the concomitant noise and public safety issues are the ones living right around the proposed base. The government should refrain from forcing its way on these people.

It seems as if the carrot-and-stick tactics of the government and the Defense Ministry were effective in dividing and conquering the Iwakuni populace. Certainly, the government and the ministry were able to remove the irksome speck in their eye by ousting Ihara from his seat and replacing him with Fukuda, a former LDP lower house member and supporter of the aircraft relocation.

However, the problems of the Iwakuni base relocation did not end with the election on February 10. Mayor Fukuda won't be able to avoid the critical gaze of much of the populace from now on. A large portion of Fukuda's supporters are likely to feel the need to repay a debt to their fellow citizens as they realize they favored the garish offers of money from the government and the Defense Ministry over the future of the city and its sense of security and safety. Also, many citizens are likely to urge Ihara to return to city government in some form. The Iwakuni problem is not finished. In fact, it's just beginning.

The US government lurks behind the Defense Ministry's moves. The problems of the Japanese government and Defense Ministry are also the problems of the US government and military.

There's something I'd like to say to the US government and the US military authorities. The Japanese government and Defense Ministry took care of business in Iwakuni with its threatening sticks and its spoiled carrots as if they were running a slave state or a feudal society. It had all the signs of a pre-modern dictatorship. The Japanese government and Defense Ministry—acting as proxies for the US government—are doing barbarous things. The US authorities should be well aware of this cruel game being played out in Iwakuni City.

The Lessons of Yubari City's Demise

During the Iwakuni mayoral election, flyers and other paraphernalia were distributed through the city claiming that if Ihara won the election, Iwakuni would be headed for the same fate as Yubari. That city's population fell from a peak of around 120,000 when the mines were operating to 12,828 in 2006, according to Wikipedia. The city's attempt to become a tourist destination—an attempt for which it borrowed heavily—failed, and the national government decided not to bail it out, forcing Yubari into bankruptcy in 2007. The following passage is from Mr. Morita's 2007 book, Amerika ni Tsukaisuterareru Nihon [America's Disposable Japan], *the second book in his trilogy on Japan's subordination to the US.*

The city of Yubari on Hokkaido is faced with a serious financial situation. On March 6, 2006, it formed an organization dedicated to rebuilding the city's finances. So why did Yubari City fall into bankruptcy? Yubari is certainly guilty of mistakes, but at the heart of the problem is Koizumi's structural reforms.

According to an article entitled "The Weath Gap Society Ten Years Later" in the February 2007 edition of _Bungei Shunju_ magazine, "In the next twenty years, Yubari City will have to pay back thirty-six billion yen, which would be the equivalent of ¥1.8 billion a year, a sum that is one-third of the city's annual budget. That means a family of four led by parents in their forties and an annual income of four million yen would see their taxes go up by ¥160,000."

The magazine article continues, "People are leaving Yubari, and the only ones left behind are the elderly and low-wage workers who can't get away ... but more than 18% of the autonomous regions around Japan could face a similar fate."

Turn-of-the-century novelist **Roka Tokutomi** was fond of saying that "a nation's potential resides in the provinces." The basic principle of politics should be to take care of these provinces. Not long ago, the very thought of a locality falling into bankruptcy would not have been tolerated. The government would have stepped in to help it avoid such a fate.

In the old days, the conventional wisdom was that if the rural areas were thriving, that would in turn energize the cities. By strengthening the provinces, both Tokyo and the outlying regions would grow together. Creating harmony between Tokyo and the provinces used to be the basic goal of Japanese politics. But Koizumi's structural reforms changed this basic premise. Instead, Koizumi opted to coolly look the other way, leaving the provinces to fend for themselves. The Abe cabinet continued the same policy. But the idea that only Tokyo needs to thrive is a dangerous one.

Kiyoshi Kuwahara is the secretary-general of an Iwakuni-based civic group called The Residents' Network to Protect the Quiet Surroundings of the Seto Inland Sea, a body of water that borders Yamaguchi Prefecture. He is in his seventies.

My wife and I have run a shop for packaging materials in Iwakuni for more than thirty years. I used to be a salesman for a company, selling the same sort of stuff. When I started out [opposing the relocation of US military aircraft to Iwakuni], our major clients left us. I expected this because the local chamber of commerce supported Yoshihiko Fukuda, who won the race. Still, I believe I'm doing the right thing.

The Iwakuni base has existed since the end of World War II. We have accepted it as it is. We have never opposed the presence of the US military.

But now we hear of the plan to expand the base's functions, doubling the number of military aircraft. Because the government has not provided us with detailed information or explanations, our concerns are growing. We don't know what the US military realignment in Japan means for us and how it relates to Japan's own defense. There has been no explanation from the Japanese government.

We usually notice the noises from the American base particularly when the weather turns bad. That is because the clouds are hanging low in the sky.

New Mayor Fukuda is telling us now that the Iwakuni base will not be expanded. But nobody believes that. As soon as Fukuda won the February race, the government dished out the much-needed money for Iwakuni. We wonder what kind of promises he made with the government, especially with Defense Minister **Shigeru Ishiba**. Although Fukuda won the race, the majority of Iwakuni residents still oppose the relocation of US military aircraft to Iwakuni.

During the election campaign, a number of women were circulating groundless rumors, saying "our hospitals are closing down" or "the city will have to stop its bus services." They were assumed to be associates of the LDP.

Iwakuni's local economy has been battered. Small and midsize businesses have been hit hard. We've been very aware of the recessionary mood. Most of us are concerned with our own economic predicaments. Our sales have been weak, dropping to just one-third of what we used to earn. As you see elsewhere in Japan, the number of part-time and temporary workers who earn less than two million yen a year has also dramatically increased in Iwakuni. They cannot get married and have a baby under such economic strain. Meanwhile, Japan continues to struggle with a low birthrate problem.

During the election campaign, contractors were very active probably because of the recession.

I like the words of former Mayor Katsusuke Ihara. He is always telling us, "A local town is run by locals, not by the central government. It is not the central government's business. We should protect our town."

Voice of the Voters III

Mutsuo Kuwahara, an Iwakuni resident in his seventies, discussed his misgivings about living close to a US military base.

During World War II, I was in Sakhalin. I was a primary school student there. I saw a number of corpses lying beside the road, but that did not scare me at all. What scared me most then was you never knew when and where bullets were going to be fired. We would dodge bullets as we fled from one place to another. I never want to go through such a horrifying experience again.

We have to remind ourselves that American soldiers here are not ordinary Americans. Their job is to kill the enemy. They are not here to help us. Their killing is legalized. Their condescending attitudes are not as different as those of the American soldiers throwing chocolates to Iwakuni citizens in this poverty-stricken city soon after the war. I continue to see the victorious nation's haughty attitudes.

Americans stationed at the Iwakuni base are very young, in their early twenties. I'm sure some of them are suffering mental anguish since they must execute their duties in the midst of high tension on foreign soil. So they let their guard down when enjoying their free time. Japan's Imperial Army soldiers would do the same. That's why tens of thousands of women, so-called **"comfort women,"** were forced to serve in Japanese military brothels.

Voice of the Voters IV: The Reluctant Radical

Kaoru Kawamoto, in her mid-fifties, lives a half mile from the US military base. She is the leader of a group of female Iwakuni residents.

I had never opposed the presence of the US military base in Iwakuni. I had never even thought of doing that. When the noise was louder, my conversation with my neighbors was just: "It sure is noisy today, isn't it?" "Yes, it is." That was all we said.

I had never wanted the government to move the base out of Iwakuni. Even when the US military caused some accidents near the base, I would say, "That was dangerous," and my friend would respond by saying, "Indeed." We wished we spoke their language to communicate with those Americans better.

But when I heard about the US military realignment plans, that changed everything. We don't need any more bases. I really want to leave Iwakuni City the way it is for our children.

My friends and I started collecting signatures. I had never done anything like this before. We ended up with sixty thousand signatures. Then we brought them to the central government with Mayor Ihara. In Tokyo, we went to several ministries including the Foreign Ministry and the Defense Ministry. I had a chance to meet a Japanese defense official, Iwao Kitahara. He looked me in the eye and told me, "We received the signatures. If something comes up, we will certainly talk to local residents first." I trusted his words completely and was very happy. Coming back to Iwakuni, I readily talked about what had happened in Tokyo with my supporters and friends. They were also pleased.

But we never heard from them again. Three months later, realignment plans were approved in a cabinet meeting. We were stunned. There was no explanation whatsoever about why the base needs to be expanded, no explanation about the realignment plans themselves.

In Iwakuni, there are various civic groups. Two of them—the Japan Council against Atomic and Hydrogen Bombs and the Japanese Trade Union Confederation—asked me to work together with them. I went to the meetings of both groups and made speeches. I could not help but feel a sense of discomfort because of the politically charged atmosphere. Once I attended their meeting, however, I felt obliged to participate in their activities all day, including cruising around the town with them, shouting political slogans.

Some of the people who supported me were shocked to see me walking with these groups. I was even asked whether I was "red." I don't think ordinary citizens who want to oppose US realignment plans can speak their minds through these groups. I no longer go to their meetings; I want my group to be a place where everyone can express themselves.

I was born and grew up in Gotsu, Shimane Prefecture. Before I got married and moved to Iwakuni, I repeatedly asked my family to bury me in the family tomb in Gotsu in the event of my death. But I have lived in Iwakuni for thirty-five years and really love it here. I like the people, the weather and the city itself though we live next to a big factory.

Many Iwakuni residents used to think matters concerning the city's military presence were something for the central government to decide. We figured that we could do nothing about it except be patient. But the current realignment plans are pushing more people to speak up now.

After Mr. Ihara became mayor, more people in the city became interested in what government does. He also tried to listen to residents, so we were gradually able to express ourselves. Still, few people would care about what the city council was discussing. After the election, however, more people watch the city council meetings on the local cable station.

Voice of the Voters V

Atsuko Himeno, in her late 40s, is an Iwakuni city councillor who used to work as a nurse.

It seems to me the economic downturn made residents desperate for whatever could turn the local economy around. Many people believed that landing some big project like construction of a civilian airport would bring in a lot of money.

The current mayor, Yoshihiko Fukuda, and I started to serve on the city council at the same time. He would often fall asleep during city council meetings. He seldom made a presentation, and even if he did, he never dealt with anything important. I really don't think he is up to the job. Many people think he was elected just because he was young and a House of Representatives member.

He became a prefectural assembly member when he was still a city councillor. Then, he was elected to the House of Representatives when he was a prefectural assembly member. And while serving as a House of Representatives member, he won the city's mayoral election.

A person like Fukuda won the election because LDP and New Komeito members launched fierce verbal attacks against former Mayor Ihara, saying loudly, "We no longer need Ihara—he goes against the government's policy."

What I have learned from the election in February is Japan has not grown into a mature democracy. Many people swallowed certain stories because they were told by an important person like a long-time city councillor. People in Yamaguchi are really conservative. The election was held amid a flurry of lies and rumors. Some people were spreading a lie that one of our hospitals would be moved to an island or a mountain-ringed region [if Ihara won]. It was obvious that it was a bluff, but it was appalling to see how many people fell for it.

People really did not understand what was going on, but they just came to believe something really bad was going to happen in Iwakuni. Some people spread lies about Mr. Ihara being a Communist Party member. The election was egregious.

Once Fukuda was elected, government leaders probably took him to their innermost sanctuary and patted him on the head. I can almost hear them saying, "We are depending on you," and Fukuda answering back, "Yes, sir."

Once the election was over, Mayor Fukuda turned his back on his campaign pledges of free school lunch and free medical bills. More people have begun to wonder what in the world the election was all about.

Ruling coalition members in the LDP and New Komeito kept saying that a new city hall wasn't being built because Ihara was acting selfishly. Many people accepted this at face value. The loudest voice won.

There was little discussion of the most important issue — US military realignment plans. Very few people understood what the issue was. The government has yet to provide much-needed information about the plans.

The media was not helpful, either. The **Yomiuri Shimbun** especially devoted more space to those who criticized Mr. Ihara. We stopped our subscription, but anonymous bloggers linked to these articles on their blogs, further spreading the rumors.

Some people were circulating the following message on the web or by email: "Iwakuni will follow in the footsteps of Yubari if nothing is done." We don't know who was doing this. But unfortunately, quite a few people believed what was written. There are many other regions where the local economy is worse than ours. Almost every region in Japan is struggling under this battered economy.

During the election campaign, I came to know many young people in their twenties and thirties who accepted at face value what was written in blogs or on websites. Some of them study at medical school. I hardly understood what they were thinking. I was taken aback by their irrelevant remarks when they said things like, "We know that if war breaks out, we will be there" [on the battlefield].

Iwakuni was a peaceful place even though the city hosts the US military. But the government's irresponsibility has divided this town. I can see resentment lingering among Iwakuni residents. We tend to identify people now as those who voted for Ihara and those who voted for Fukuda.

The Diagnosis

CHAPTER 8

STOPPING THE KC

*Peace is the only moral value
that matters in the pursuit of truth.
But human society has only known
the morality of oppression
and resignation.*

— ROMAIN ROLLAND

FOR A FIVE-AND-A-HALF YEAR SPAN FROM SPRING 2001 TO autumn 2006, Japan's mass media hyped and supported the Koizumi administration in a way that resembles the Cultural Revolution of Mao Zedong, which swept through China in the 1960s and 70s. The Japanese people, much like the Chinese during their revolution, joined in the frenzied adulation.

Mao's Cultural Revolution brought about the huge fantasy of Mao-style Communism, and the Chinese people joined in the dance of social destruction. The goal of the Koizumi Cultural Revolution was to Americanize Japan. Or more precisely, it was to bring about Republican-style Americanization of Japan.

The true leader of the Koizumi Cultural Revolution was US President George W. Bush. Koizumi tried to remodel Japan into a country that embraced Bush's Republican-style politics. The former prime minister was supported in his efforts by the Liberal Democratic Party, New Komeito, Soka Gakkai, government officials, the financial sector and the mass media.

But the media was the most adoring. It became an arm of the Koizumi administration. News outlets were like hit men for the **UMI REVOLUTION** administration, taking down all its critics. TV stations were Koizumi's minions doing the bidding of the politically powerful.

How did the TV stations become so corrupt? Because they live by commercials. Most of the commercials are financed by companies with foreign capital. The thing that moves Dentsu, the pinnacle of the Japanese advertising world, is foreign capital. Japanese TV is manipulated by foreign capital. Just about anything disagreeable to the foreign capital that controls Japanese TV is kept off the air. Programs that criticize the US are censored and tossed aside. It's quite similar to the situation under the **Occupation**, when a publishing company that dared to criticize the US would be run out of business, but it's still shocking to consider that this is the situation in the twenty-first century. It is also common knowledge that coverage of crimes by American soldiers has been decreasing.

Newspapers are supported by ads too. The thing we should worry about when we pick up our daily newspaper is not what is written in it, but what is *not* written in it. The same goes for TV.

In my view, Koizumi was the most irresponsible and frivolous prime minister in Japan's postwar history. The former premier took a stable

Japan and destroyed it; after it began to collapse, he walked away from the destruction like a triumphant shogun. Koizumi's politics left behind a giant legacy that is weighing on the backs of the populace.

For the opposition parties in the Diet, there will never be a better chance to seize control. A change of administration is possible if the Democratic Party of Japan, the central party of the opposition, is able to bring the other opposition parties together and present a united front. However, I worry about the caliber of the DPJ's leadership.

Bills that were passed as part of Koizumi's structural reforms have recently come into effect. This is an important point. Postal privatization laws went into effect in fall 2007. Corporate reforms started in April of that year. Tax cuts were halted in January 2007. The severe effects of Koizumi's reforms are just beginning to be felt by Japan's citizens. The destruction of the tax base, the medical system, education and farming will only accelerate.

The message I would especially like to get across in this book is that the structural reforms instituted during the five and a half years of the Koizumi administration are at the root of the ills plaguing modern Japan. In the following chapters, I would like to explain in more detail how Koizumi's revolution is destroying Japan.

CHAPTER 9

AMERICANIZING JAPAN'S ECONOMY:
THE TRUTH BEHIND

In early 2007, the Japanese Diet was very close to passing something known as the "white-collar exemption," which would have eliminated overtime pay for white-collar workers. The idea has since been tabled, but many analysts believe the bill will be reintroduced at the proper time. Mr. Morita wrote the following passage as the Diet got ready to pass the bill in January 2007.

THIS "WHITE-COLLAR EXEMPTION" IS A SIGN OF THE Americanization—and the destruction—of the Japanese economy. It only benefits companies with foreign capital and domestic companies that are willing to be Americanized.

This exemption didn't just spring out of nowhere. It began back in June 2001, when Koizumi and Bush held a bilateral meeting where they announced the US-Japan Economic Partnership for Growth.

The two countries agreed to establish something called the Investment Initiative, which came out of talks between the two leaders on what measures were needed to improve investment opportunities.

On the surface, this was a mutual agreement, but in reality it was a one-way deal that Koizumi was pressured into making. One of the American demands in the talks was that Japan adopt this so-called white-collar exemption.

In June 2006, the US State Department and the Japanese Ministry

E LABOR BIG BANG

of Economy, Trade and Industry (METI) published the US-Japan Investment Initiative Report. Here is part of that report:

> The Government of the United States suggested that improving labor mobility would be a key to maximize the value of organizations, highlighting the following: ... Introduce a white-collar exemption that would replace the working hours scheme for supervisory and managerial employees under the Labor Standards Act, in order to better foster workers' abilities.

The Americans were simply trying to Americanize Japan's economy. The white-collar exemption is an unjustified attempt to take away the rights of managers, specialists and other white-collar workers.

Koizumi's structural reforms have brought to an end Japan's **"hundred million middle class"** society. Abe and those who followed him only furthered the dream of making Japan a US colony, pushing Japan closer to a society of "hundred million captives."

The administrations of Koizumi and Abe have brought us an

Americanized Japan. Those under the influence of American propaganda — the national newspaper reporters, TV anchors, corporate executives, bureaucrats and academics — have only furthered the cause. The Japanese economy is becoming Americanized — the nightmare is real and happening now.

The idea that everything American is good and that Japan should just follow along is an odd one indeed. In fact, it's the height of madness. Japan's politicians, bureaucrats, financiers, academics and media personalities are all caught up in this madness. If you think about it with a clear mind, the idea of Americanizing Japan — like trying to blend trees with bamboo — is just plain nonsense. But that is exactly what is happening to Japan's economy and its system of laws.

Americanization Means More Katakana in Official Business

The Japanese language is made up of three syllabary: hiragana, katakana *and* kanji, *or Chinese characters.* Katakana *is used for foreign or loan words. So a hamburger is rendered* hanbagaa *in* katakana. *In this section, Mr. Morita notes that use of* katakana *has spread far beyond the fast-food menu.*

Former Prime Minister Abe was fond of calling Japan a "beautiful country," but ever since his administration took over, there has been a flood of *katakana* used in official meetings: Ajia Geetouei (Asia Gateway), Inobueeshyon 25 (Innovation 25), Sai-Chyarenji (Re-Challenge) ... The list goes on. This is also an example of the Americanization of Japan.

If the elite class in Japan dons any more American habits, we'll soon be writing our official documents in English. I've heard that some academics think it's a good idea to make English the official language for government business. I oppose this current trend in Americanization.

I'm against the white-collar exemption, but if they are going to make it into a law, the least they could do is render it in Japanese.

A Society with No Choices

One way to measure economic progress is through a country's gross domestic product, or GDP. This GDP accounts for about one-fifth to one-sixth of a nation's wealth. A nation's wealth is based on the value of its assets at a given time, so the citizens' debt is subtracted from their assets. That's a nation's wealth, and I think it's a truer indication of a nation's economic health.

Before World War II, Japan's wealth peaked in 1936, the year of the attempted coup d'etat known as the **February 26th Incident.** Japan prepared itself for war the following year, and at first Japan was victorious and its wealth did not decrease.

However, Japan's wealth dropped rapidly in the two years beginning in 1943. In fact, it plunged by about 30%. After the **US firebombings** of Osaka, Tokyo and other large cities in the war years, Japan's wealth in 1945 had dropped to about 70% of what it was in 1936.

It took about twenty-five years to regain that lost 30%. Even with the fast-paced economic reconstruction of the postwar years, it took until 1970 to return to the level Japan had seen in 1936. That was the result of years of sweat and toil by Japan's workers.

For some reason today, the government doesn't make public the nation's wealth. While there are no exact figures to pore over, it is safe to say that Japan's wealth has greatly decreased as a result of Koizumi's structural reforms. Japan continued to sink economically during his five and a half years in office. It is going to take a lot of time and effort to repair the loss.

The main policy of the Meiji government (1868–1912) was "wealthy country, strong military." The aim of the nation was to build wealth and make sure the military was robust. This policy stayed in place until Japan lost the war in 1945. After the war, the nation let go of the need for a strong military and concentrated on building wealth.

But in the twenty-first century, Japan has lost its focus on building wealth. Japan has become a nation without a goal. This is a serious problem. Following the path laid out by Bush's Republican Party, Japan lost its goals as it pursued Koizumi's reforms.

A January 13, 2007, article in the *Yomiuri Shimbun*, Japan's largest daily newspaper, highlighted a government report on the economic state of Japan's households in fiscal 2005. The report showed that households had saved just 3.1% of their disposable income during that year, down 0.3 percentage point from the previous year. Savings rates had fallen for eight consecutive years, the report said, and were just one-seventh what they were at the peak in 1975, when an average Japanese household saved 23.1% of its disposable income.

If this trend continues, it will be impossible to avert an increase of more unhappy people in Japan. The nation has become a place without a future, without a goal. There is an increased possibility that as morals continue to decay, the society will start to crumble. Fixing these problems won't be easy.

But it must be said that we aren't out of options yet. If the Japanese people find the will to rebuild and get in touch with that which makes this country special, we can recover.

First, we have to make the politicians take responsibility for letting Japan fall so sharply; we must punish the treasonous ones by voting them out of office. One of the reasons Japan was able to stand again after World War II was that people were held responsible for their crimes. The Japanese people repudiated war and lived in peace for sixty years. A second round of justice for the latest crimes — the destroying of Japanese society and the dashing of any sort of hope at the bidding of the Americans—should be vigorously enforced. This would lead to a new era filled with a new sort of hope.

JAPAN'S HOUSEHOLD SAVINGS RATE (1975–2006)

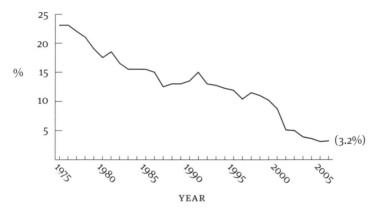

(Source: Japanese government statistics)

Wealth Gap No Secret to Japanese

Around the end of 2006, I visited a bookstore near Meguro Station in Tokyo and saw firsthand how in the last two or three years there have been a lot of books published about the growing economic gap in society. Several were even best sellers.

I believe that this trend of books criticizing the path Japan is on — the path set by Bush and Koizumi — is only going to strengthen.

At the same time, while all the books are well-written and interesting, almost none of them focus on the real origins of this wealth gap—namely, the colonization of Japan and the way the Japanese government obediently follows the path the US sets for it. Editors and publishers don't have a very strong sense of the necessity to attack Koizumi's structural revolution head on. Or perhaps more to the point, people are afraid of criticizing the Koizumi administration. Even today, the remnants of six years of unadulterated praise for Junichiro Koizumi is not easy to shake.

The mass media's unabashed promotion of the Koizumi administration has taken root in the public mind. The power of media is stunning to behold. And frightening. It turned this villain called Koizumi into a hero.

The wealth gap was made by the Koizumi cabinet at the behest of the Bush administration, which is keen on making Japan's economy more American. They had help from the LDP-Komeito ruling coalition, elite bureaucrats, leaders of the economic sphere, pro-American academics and the media. The Japanese mass media should be analyzing and explaining this problem, but it runs away from it, able only to report on what is directly in front of it, which is a shame.

The Japanese publishing industry must fulfill its role of analyzing the wealth gap. We must begin a real critique of the Koizumi structural revolution. Japanese journalism really crashed and burned when it turned the worst, most sycophantic American follower in Japanese political history and his puppet government into heroes. This is especially true with political journalism. This legacy must be corrected.

I've read dozens of books that tackle the wealth gap, but I'm always left feeling that they just scratch the surface. What's missing is the analysis and search for just who and what turned Japan into this pathetic version of itself.

How do we go about punishing those responsible? The answer: Regime change. We need to throw out the politicians responsible for this mess and bring in some new political leadership.

CHAPTER 10

EXPLOITED

W HAT JAPAN IS EXPERIENCING TODAY IS NOT A WEALTH
gap, but the manifestations of a class society. That's how
rapidly the social and economic chasm has widened.

The government has announced that Japan's economic recovery
since 2002 has continued for fifty-nine months straight as of December 2006 and continues at a record-breaking pace, surpassing the
fifty-seven-month record set during the period of high economic
growth in the 1960s and 1970s. But regular Japanese folks are not
touched by this supposed prosperity. On the contrary, an increasing
number of people are noticing the economic gap between the haves
and the have-nots.

A survey conducted in January 2007 by the *Yomiuri Shimbun*
posed this question: "Do you feel that Japan has become a society
with a wealth gap?" Ninety-one percent responded, "Yes."

How did Japan become such a society?

After the war, Japan managed to create an egalitarian society and a massive middle class—a rarity for a capitalist system—through a successful and sustained period of economic growth. Then in 1992, the US government suggested an exchange of policy recommendations — the US-Japan Regulatory Reform and Competition Policy Initiative—to then Prime Minister Miyazawa. He agreed to the idea.

ENTRAPPED

The US government was intent on reshaping Japan's structure to suit its own needs. The recommendations eventually became, in effect, the blueprint for fiscal reform in Japan. Starting with the Murayama cabinet (1994–96), the US government has pointed to the initiative and applied political pressure on Japan to comply with it.

The Koizumi administration strongly pushed for reforms when its term began in April 2001. Due to Koizumi's reforms, Japan's middle class began to crumble, and money stopped flowing into smaller, regional economies, leading to their collapse. The result today is a fragmented society of haves and have-nots.

The Koizumi administration has caused much suffering for the Japanese people while creating a society that delivers profits to the US government and big businesses. The proud Japanese accomplishment known as the massive middle class has been destroyed, and that is the legacy of the Koizumi reforms.

The Koizumi and Abe administrations are treating the widening gap in Japanese society as if it were some sort of natural phenomenon. They have been concealing the fact that the government is directly responsible for it.

* * *

I get so many comments on the widening wealth gap from readers of my website. Here's one:

Lately, I've noticed that the mass media is using the term "wealth gap" with growing frequency. I've always had a little problem with that phrase. When the media, which has virtually become one with the government, throws around phrases like, "The widening wealth gap must be addressed," or "The gap must be lessened," that's because such expressions mean so little to the ruling class. They haven't even begun to address the severity of the issue.

This is what's happening to this country right now: the ruling coalition, which sold its soul to America for its own profit, is stealing from its own people. In other words, laborers are being increasingly suppressed and exploited by big capital.

Labor unions are being quashed or bought out by big money. So, now that they are no longer functional, the ruling class is doing as it pleases.

Seeking a classless society is like asking for the removal of inequities. That's why the government has resorted to the use of deceptive phrases, such as "Renewing the Challenge."

This is no light matter. The lives of citizens are at stake. People can't make a living, get hospital treatment nor find a hospital to give birth. Their rehabilitation programs are being cancelled and their very lives are at stake.

A healthy media would demand that the government protect the lives of its citizens, not talk about the wealth gap in such ambiguous terms that don't address culpability. They should be confronting the government, challenging things like the labor dispatch system or preferential treatment of big corporations.

We already have a country that operates on the notion that it can mass-produce the poor and force young people to join the military and go off to fight on a battlefield somewhere. That would be the US. Is it too cynical then to think that the mass production of the working poor in Japan may be just another order handed down from the US? Not necessarily. Frankly speaking, moves such as revisions to the **Fundamental Law of Education**, the establishment of the **Defense Ministry** and **constitutional revisions** reek of gunpowder. Here, too, is the great issue of human life. We are no longer talking about the differences between the rich and the poor in a class society; this is fundamentally about the battle between those who take life versus those whose lives are taken from them. Mass media must inform Japanese citizens of the truth.

Fellow journalists: No matter how much you align yourselves with the authorities, when war is declared, your sons will be sent to the battlefield. The only exceptions are made for a few privileged statesmen, which is so obvious it does not need to be mentioned.

Your mission is to speak the truth to the citizens of Japan and help save them from disasters, is it not?

CHAPTER 11

EMERGENCE OF T

*For sorrow ends
not when it seemeth done.*

— WILLIAM SHAKESPEARE

THE WORDS ON THE COVER OF THE JUNE 19, 2007, EDITION of the **Shukan Economist** magazine carried impact: "The Wretched Workplace of Our Daughters and Sons: Even when married, nonpermanent employees barely get by."

The article is a serious piece. It introduces a serious reality in Japan today—namely, the emergence of the working poor.

An old friend and former member of the House of Councillors, Yasuo Yamashita, invited me to give a lecture at a local labor union conference in Seki City, Gifu Prefecture, on June 14, 2007. While I was there, I heard the following: Of the union members in the Seki area, one-third have regular employment, another third have non-regular work (contract workers, part-timers) and another third are foreign workers. The foreigners face the most severe work conditions, people said. The non-regular workers get little pay, and no matter how hard they work, they can't escape from debt. They are Japan's working poor, a class of people that is growing rapidly.

In the *Shukan Economist* article, Miki Kobayashi, a journalist specializing in labor economics, writes about HIKS (half income with kids) couples:

WORKING POOR

"Once I got married and pregnant, I had no choice but to resign from my work, and our family income dropped by half. My husband's work is also unstable. Even if we want a second child, we can't have one," says twenty-nine-year-old Akemi Takeuchi, the mother of a six-year-old daughter. People around the age of thirty have come to be known as the Employment Ice Age Generation because they have seen a series of recessions freezing employment. This is the age when people start marrying and having families, but this generation lives amid difficult times.

The economic power of the Ice Age Generation has weakened just as its members enter the age for marriage and childbirth.

The number of non-regular employees in Japan has reached 16.77 million, up 440,000 in just six months. The percentage of non-regular employees has hit a new high, and the trend toward non-regular employment has not been slowed.

We have to rescue the twenty- and thirty-something working poor. Basically, this is the responsibility of the government, but the ruling coalition isn't even close to treating this problem with the full seriousness it deserves. This administration doesn't do full seriousness.

To save those in their twenties and thirties, we need a reversal of political power and a change of administration. And we can't afford to lose.

No Matter How Hard They Work ...

The Koizumi reforms have created great chasms in three areas: regions, businesses and livelihoods.

1. The regional gap is manifested in the way wealth pours only into Tokyo; cities, towns and villages in outlying areas crumble from neglect.
2. The business gap refers to the advantages that flow toward big corporations. Small to midsize companies can barely stay afloat.
3. The small increase in the wealthy class is overwhelmed by a sharp rise in the poor.

Japan's current population is about 127 million. Twenty million of the total are relatively wealthy; fifty million are in the middle class, caught in a gentle downward spiral; and the remaining sixty million live in poverty. The fifty million in the middle are rapidly splitting apart: a small minority is upwardly mobile, and the rest are joining the ranks of the working poor, who struggle to make ends meet.

A survey by the Ministry of Internal Affairs and Communications showed that there were 6.87 million workers between the ages of fifteen and thirty-four who were earning less than two million yen, or about twenty thousand dollars, a year. The trend is toward an increase in the number of young people who work and work and work but can't make their lives any easier. In fact, the harder you work, the tougher your life. This is a serious issue that can't be ignored anymore.

An interview with Uichiro Niwa, member of the government-appointed Council on Economic and Fiscal Policy and chairman of Itochu Corp., ran in the February 4, 2007, issue of the *Yomiuri Shimbun*. Here's what he had to say about raising the minimum wage for workers and closing the wealth gap:

> If you look at Japan's minimum wage, there's only been a 7% increase per hour over the past ten years. It is miserable compared with increases of 37–52% in countries such as the US, UK and France. The region with the highest minimum wage is Tokyo, at ¥719 per hour. The lowest are Aomori and Iwate prefectures and Okinawa at ¥610 per hour. The weighted national average is ¥673. This comes out to earnings of ¥118,448 a month [about $1,200] after working eight hours a day, twenty-two days of the month.

But this type of viewpoint is not reflected in the work of the Council on Economic and Fiscal Policy. In the February 2007 issue of **Bungei Shunju**, a high-profile news magazine, Niwa talked about the class society and where it will be ten years later. He said that the number of young workers in their twenties who make less than ¥1.5 million a year has increased by 6.5% over the last ten years. Those who have part-time or temp jobs can work all they want but will remain below the welfare line, always working and always poor. In November 2006, the council freed companies from legal employment obligations to temp workers under certain conditions. Now employers can freely fire people who are not full-time employees.

The council chairman is Prime Minister Yasuo Fukuda. Other members include Chief Cabinet Secretary Nobutaka Machimura, Minister of State for Economic and Fiscal Policy Hiroko Ota, Minister of Internal Affairs and Communications Hiroya Masuda, Canon Inc.

Chairman Fujio Mitarai and Naohiro Yashiro, economist and professor at International Christian University.

The council is made up of cabinet members, heads of major corporations and scholars that are patronized by the government—in other words, a group of people who couldn't possibly develop policies that are sympathetic toward the struggles of the Japanese people even if their lives depended on it.

Letters on the Working Poor

I receive many letters from readers on this issue and would like to share two that are representative of the bulk of the feedback I've received.

December 10, 2006

Dear Mr. Morita,

Yesterday I watched the **NHK** TV special called "Working Poor II." It was an excellent program that portrayed how women and senior citizens who are willing to work hard still could not move out of poverty.

There was a divorced mother who was trying to raise her young child while working a job that paid six hundred yen [about six dollars] an hour. There was also a young girl who should have been in high school furthering her education but had to work a job that paid ¥650 an hour to support her family because her father was ill. Then an old man had to pick up cans in the park for money to support himself and his wife because they had no pension; they were forced to spend it all when they ran out of money. They had saved ¥700,000 for their funerals, but he scraped by on fifty thousand yen a month from finding recyclable cans. He was eighty and she was seventy-five.

The program sharply criticized this trend in our society.

I am writing to you, Mr. Morita, to tell you what some viewers think of the show.

An NHK official in charge of the program told the National Confederation of Trade Unions that whenever the station airs the show, they are flooded with calls by people saying, "How long are you going to run this show? It's their own fault that those people are poor."

This afternoon, I overheard the following conversation at lunch between two **salarymen**. One of the men was passionately talking to the other about the show. "Does this country want to tell those people to go off and die or what?" said the man. He was really worked up about it.

This is the average response from most people who watched the show, I believe.

So what's with all the phone calls to NHK complaining about the show? I am forced to believe that this is an organized and funded attempt to annoy NHK. I believe that rich people are behind this attack on the media's conscience.

Dear Mr. Morita,

I watched NHK's "Working Poor II," which aired on December 10. The program introduced various stories, including an eighty-year-old man who had to earn a living by collecting cans in the park; a seventy-five-year-old man whose monthly pension of sixty thousand yen went to the hospital to pay for his wife, who was hospitalized with a cognitive disease, and forced him to work in park maintenance for money; and a thirty-one-year old mother who tried to raise her twelve- and ten-year-old boys while working part-time jobs both day and night. The government has reformed medical care and cut child care to the point where it is depriving people in need from their right to live a normal life.

What is difficult to swallow is that when a societal problem like the working poor emerges, these people don't lend a hand to those in need; rather, they cut provisions ... Has there ever been an era sadder than the one we're living through where the politicians were so cold-blooded to the populace? I cannot say.

Koizumi's excessive reforms have brought about a competitive society, creating a larger underclass that can't work its way out of poverty. What is so beautiful [a reference to former Prime Minister Abe's penchant for calling Japan a "beautiful country"] about a country where people work and work and still aren't allowed to live like human beings? Politicians need to realize that they perpetuate a politics that doesn't deal with reality and a political culture that ignores the citizens.

Putting a Financial Squeeze on the Elderly

The Koizumi administration's ill-conceived reforms of the national pension system don't just affect the working poor. By reducing the amount of social insurance, the onus on senior citizens is increased. Deductions have been abolished for the elderly and minimized for those living off their pensions. Here's a snippet from the June 18, 2006, **Asahi Shimbun**, a national newspaper, that illustrates this point:

> The tax reform that occurred in fiscal 2004, which includes the end of additional deductions on one's public pension and the

abolishment of deductions for the elderly, results in a skyrocketing residence tax burden for the average seventy-six-year-old man, from four thousand yen in fiscal 2005 to ¥31,100 in fiscal 2006.

Moreover, in fiscal 2008, with new medical reforms kicking in, seniors will be expected to pay an average of ¥61,000 in insurance. By fiscal 2015, that burden will rise to ¥85,000. The costs of medical care are escalating. When you're healthy, you can earn an income, but for those senior citizens who are living off just their pensions, the distress is palpable.

The abolishment of the fixed-rate tax reduction, ushered in during the administration of Keizo Obuchi, really hurts the working class. For a family of four (husband, wife and two children) where the parents are making an income of three million yen, the tax burden goes up seven hundred yen. If that family makes five million yen, the extra tax is ¥17,600, and if the family makes seven million yen, its tax bill jumps by ¥41,000. The gradual phasing out of the tax reduction started in fiscal 2007 with the abolishment of a parental tax break that will impact households with children younger than fifteen.

Until now, a family with one child would get a subsidy of about twenty thousand yen. But thanks to the Koizumi reforms, subsidies were completely eliminated in fiscal 2007 for families with children between the ages of sixteen and eighteen. A survey conducted in fiscal 2003 on the number of households led by a mother with children showed a twenty-eight percent increase over five years to 1.23 million households.

Politicians should have as their goal the easing of the citizens' tax burden. But the government rationalizes its moves by saying, "The fixed-rate tax reduction was a temporary measure, so we're just returning it to normal." The ruling parties obstinately insist that this doesn't amount to a tax hike; they behave like royalty wielding unchecked authority.

When the Obuchi cabinet unveiled its plan for a fixed-rate tax reduction, it was part of a package that also lowered the highest individual and corporate tax brackets. Of these three measures, only the fixed-rate tax reduction is being rolled back; only the average citizen is expected to shoulder the burden of higher taxes.

The tax breaks for the rich continue. The corporate tax burden has lessened further. Is this the way it should be? The government's stance on this issue is fundamentally flawed.

There's Still Time to Stop These Misguided and Bad Laws

If we can bring about political change, we can stop all these bad laws—abolishment of the fixed-rate tax reduction, deductions for the elderly and families, and postal privatization. We need to push for a dissolution of the lower house and a general election as soon as possible.

Despite the victory by the opposition in the July 2007 upper-house elections, it is difficult to roll back laws without control of the lower house. We need a general election to bring about basic changes in the political landscape.

Finally, allow me to introduce one piece of evidence on the ill effects of postal privatization.

A while back, I was delivering a lecture on Kyushu. At a party that followed, I had a conversation with a woman whose family ran a vending machine business. This woman told me that the post office had decided to get rid of all its vending machines and replace them with vending machines sold by an American company. This is how postal privatization will play out.

Another theory has an enormous amount of funds in Japan's postal life insurance circulating through American brokerage Goldman Sachs and buying thirty-year US government bonds. If this is true, it would be a huge development.

But it's not yet too late to change all this. We can still fix these laws. By voting out the current ruling politicians in the next election, a new government could review these laws with a new set of priorities. If we have the will, we can reverse these laws. If we don't, Japan will continue its collapse. Everything depends on the consciousness of the Japanese people.

CHAPTER 12

THE ARROGANCE ANI

L ATELY THE FINANCIAL SECTOR, ESPECIALLY **KEIDANREN**
(the Japan Federation of Economic Organizations), has become increasingly tyrannical. Some critics call Keidanren
"Baikokuren," using the characters for selling (*bai*) the country
(*koku*). The financial sector has switched into survival mode. That
is, its survival is tantamount; nothing else — the people, the small to
midsize firms — matters.

Keidanren is promoting a tax hike on consumption after having
convinced the government to reduce corporate taxes. This is none
other than mass robbery. Politics is for the people. Business management must also be for the people.

Japanese business leaders used to have a strong sense of mission toward society and the people within it. They believed that they
were working for the greater good of the people.

Few business leaders think in those terms anymore. They are concerned only about themselves and their companies' profits. Their philosophy is: "All's well if it serves me. You got a problem with that?" This is how soulless Japan's business leaders have become. These ego-driven business leaders are of no value to the Japanese people.

I would like to make a suggestion: how about if Keidanren Chairman **Fujio Mitarai** and other leaders of Japan's largest corporations all move to the United States? Japan doesn't need business leaders of

YOPIA OF KEIDANREN

their kind—hawkers who try to sell Japan's wealth to America.

I have this to say to Toyota Motor Corp., a major corporation that represents Japan around the world:

In Nagoya, I rode a taxi and asked the driver: "Newspapers and magazines in Tokyo frequently comment on the upbeat Nagoya economy. How are you all doing?"

The driver practically spat out his reply: "Are you kidding? There are no passengers in Nagoya who would ride a taxi after 8 pm. Things are really very difficult for us now."

His anger was palpable. "Newspapers in Tokyo write that Nagoya is doing well just because Toyota is doing well, but the company's gotten fat from sucking every little bit from us."

I attended a party hosted by Nagoya business leaders. Here are some comments overheard at the party: "Business is extremely difficult," "We're being tightly squeezed," "They're being really harsh to subcontractors," "We can't survive without Toyota," "We sell even if we know we'll lose money in the deal," "The more we work, the bigger our debts."

Behind Every Victorious Shogun are Ten Thousand Dead Soldiers

At a local government meeting, I commented on Aichi Prefecture's robust economy. One business owner replied, "You must be joking. Toyota is the only one doing well. There's nothing positive for us now. We've all become a human sacrifice for Toyota. What goes on today in Aichi Prefecture can be summed up in this proverb: 'Behind every victorious shogun are ten thousand dead soldiers.'"

In others areas, like Tahara, Toyota has been a savior.

The two towns of Atsumi and Tahara merged to create Tahara City. In the union, the famous "Atsumi" moniker was dropped. Tahara was kept because Toyota's factory is located in Tahara.

Toyota employees populate Tahara, bringing prosperity to the city. Tax revenues increase. Tahara residents are grateful—it's all thanks to Toyota.

At the same time, some small-business owners in Japan have been driven to suicide because of their mounting debts.

Toyota as a group has about 280,000 full-time employees. Another 100,000 employees are not full-time. Japan's overall work force is reflective of that. The percentage of part-time employees is 33%. I'd like to see Toyota, as a leading Japanese firm, adopt a more humanitarian employment practice.

A Corporate Windfall: Tax Exemptions for Exporters

Keidanren insists that without a 2% increase in the consumption tax, the country will run up against a primary deficit. Toyota, Canon Inc., Sony Corp., Matsushita Electric Industrial Co.—among other export giants—are all in agreement over this.

A tax hike amid floundering consumption is extremely dangerous to Japan's current economy. A sharp drop in consumption can potentially trigger panic.

Does Keidanren not see that a tax hike would cool demand for goods and drag consumption into a downward spiral? Perhaps exporters do not understand the significance of domestic consumption's impact on the economy.

Exporters make up the core of Keidanren. There must be some serious lobbying from the exporters behind Keidanren's demands for a consumption-tax increase.

The National Tax Agency website explains that exporters get the full amount of any consumption tax reimbursed to them along with other write-offs and refunds. Some say this is the reason behind Keidanren's push for a higher consumption tax. And if that's the case, the consumption tax is really about cashing in.

The Impoverished Many and the Prosperous Few

Corporate tax decreases and export exemptions are a boon to big companies with international markets. Our country's economic policies have protected the export business at the expense of the people.

Big corporations and the coalition government are entrapping the Japanese people so that their riches can be sucked dry according to the wishes of the American government. We are creating a slave society where only big corporations and foreign capital will thrive. We're transitioning from a massive middle class to a massive society of indentured servants.

Japan's decision to align itself with the Reagan Administration unleashed within Japan a financial beast with an insatiable appetite that put pressure on the government willy-nilly. It is around this time, too, that the Japanese government's economic policies began to show heavy favoritism toward big corporations, and Japanese and American capitalism developed into its current co-dependency. In other words, the Japanese economy became vulnerable to the growing influence of US firms in Japan.

As the American brand of capitalism strengthened its hold in Japan, the stage was set for the Darwinian theory to prevail; only the strongest and the biggest of the companies were to reap all the benefits. The **Council on Economic and Fiscal Policy** added a member from the financial sector during the Koizumi years. For the financial sector, this was a political victory, a share of the political power. Leaders of big corporations banded with the Koizumi administration to subjugate themselves to American rule and prey on Japan.

Big business owners have only their profit in mind. It's as if the people of Japan mean nothing to them. Their interest is solely in cashing in as much as they can. While I wish I could say otherwise, this is no exaggeration.

I have received letters from readers expressing anger toward Keidanren and its skewed system, and the way big corporations treat their employees. Let me introduce one:

Dear Mr. Morita,

I'd like to comment on the economic rejuvenation policy. Fortunately, Japan's economy is robust, thanks to big corporate profits and the resulting increase in tax revenues. The problem lies with private spending or a lack thereof. The reason for that is simply a decline in labor's share of national income. According to a survey by the *Nihon Keizai Shimbun*, bonuses given out in fiscal 2005 made up 1.98% of the nation's income. Reliable statistics beyond that were hard to find, but I have to assume that corporate operating profits are well above those figures.

The workers at Toyota demanded a pay raise that would have come out to a total cost to the company of ¥500 million a year. Keidanren was unanimous in its reluctance to support this proposition.

Among the many causes of Japan's slump is a lack of any economic wiggle room for individuals. This situation could be reversed if a portion of corporate profits could be diverted toward bonuses or wages. Here's why:

1. Wage increases will promote greater spending.
2. Increased personal spending means greater circulation of cash, a boost to the economy and a rise in stock prices.
3. Economic prosperity at an individual level leads to a greater sense of spiritual and financial stability, thereby contributing to the well being of society as a whole.
4. The increased wages result in increased tax revenues, which in turn promote a healthier economy.

Discussions on wage increases usually take place in spring, but there is no law making this so. Can the prime minister appeal to corporations to share their profits with their employees to reinvigorate the economy? If he doesn't take action, perhaps the opposition parties can take up the cause. Fortunately, corporations have cash to spend in Japan. Instead of viewing an increase in labor costs as a worker's right, consider it a tool to help support the economy, as the first step toward economic expansion. That makes economic rejuvenation a viable goal.

Years ago, it was not uncommon for hardworking businessmen in Japan to earn ten million yen a year with the support of the seniority and lifetime employment systems. Today, no matter how hard one works, one cannot earn more than seven million yen a year working at a small to midsize company. Severe wage restrictions and a performance-oriented system were adopted by the government and the financial sector. This performance-based system is wrecking the Japanese economy, in my opinion.

A businessman's high salary has as much to do with luck as ability. Ability and luck go hand in hand to bring about good results. Good fortune tends to fall upon those who work hard, for sure, but to base monetary rewards too much on performance is dangerous.

So how does one draw the line between luck and ability? Through promotion. Placing an individual in the appropriate position will help an organization move smoothly. Give the individual an executive post, then allow him or her administrative allowances.

Many employees will lose motivation when they learn that they are making less than their colleagues.

I often hear that a performance-based system can be detrimental to companies of about five hundred or so employees—that it actually hurts performance.

An American-style merit system is unsuitable to Japan, a country that has stressed egalitarianism with great success. Imagine forcing that system onto small and midsize companies. Failure is most certain; this is where Japan has made a big mistake.

This mistake must be reckoned with and fixed.

CHAPTER 13

POSTAL PRIVATIZ

T HANKS TO THE KOIZUMI CABINET'S STRONG EFFORTS TO push postal privatization on the public, the fate of Japanese assets will soon be in the hands of foreign investors.

Back on August, 8, 2005, then Prime Minister Koizumi dissolved the lower house after lawmakers in the upper house refused to pass bills supporting postal privatization. At the time, I viewed this dissolution as unconstitutional.

The day after the lower-house dissolution, I appeared on TV and made the following statement: "Prime Minister Koizumi's decision to dissolve the lower house is a misuse of the prime minister's authority and thus is unconstitutional." I heard much later that the TV network was sharply reprimanded by government authorities and members of the ruling Liberal Democratic Party. After my comment, the TV network severed its ties with me. It was their way of suppressing my speech.

A month later, on September 11, the media reported an overwhelming victory in the general election for Koizumi's LDP and its coalition partner, New Komeito. In an extraordinary Diet session after the elections, the subject of postal privatization was revisited, and by October 14, the bills had been submitted and approved by the Diet.

The privatization of Japan's postal services is supposed to be phased in over ten years beginning in October 2007 and reaching

completion in October 2017. But even before this process started, privatization quickly was becoming a fait accompli.

Take the delivery of the New Year's postcards in 2007. Japan's postal service reported that about seven million cards were delivered late. I live in the Shiroganedai neighborhood in Tokyo's Minato Ward, a central location, and I had the distinct impression that the delivery was a little off. I've never had this low level of service in the fifty years that I have lived here. A friend told me that he sent a New Year's postcard to a friend in the provinces and it still hadn't arrived a week later. This sort of thing didn't happen before; these small occurrences show that the postal service in Japan is slipping.

The major newspapers all published letters from readers complaining about the poor postal service around New Year's Day. **Masaharu Ikuta**, then president of the **Japan Post**, held a press conference on January 17 to explain the situation. Here's what he said according to a report that ran on the **Kyodo** wire:

"All the postcards we received by December 28 were delivered on New Year's Day," Ikuta said. But because mail volume was up after December 26, he went on to explain, the sorting was late, and just thirty percent of the postcards received on December 29 were delivered on January 1, down from the usual rate of eighty percent.

The Japan Postal Agency estimated that there were 3.62 billion New Year's postcards featuring traditional *otoshi-dama* cash gifts, down 3.7% from the previous year.

I'm guessing that not too many people felt appeased by Mr. Ikuta's comments. A friend who is knowledgeable about the inner workings of the postal system told me that one of the managers involved with the postcard deliveries straightforwardly apologized and said he and other managers take responsibility for the poor performance. That's quite a long way from Ikuta's quibbling response. And it's clear which one was telling the truth. The post office was in serious disarray over the New Year holidays.

The government repeats its mantra that the privatization of postal services hasn't and won't reduce services. It's a bald-faced lie. The reality is quite different. The quality of service is actually dropping rapidly.

Not so long ago, public entities were plentiful in Japan: Each town and village had government offices; agricultural cooperatives flourished; and public railroad stations and local branches of the telephone company were the norm. But under former Prime Minister Yasuhiro Nakasone, the public train stations and phone company offices began to disappear. The recent past has left the post office as the sole public outlet in many provinces. But now, with postal privatization, these outposts are disappearing too. People sometimes say that only police stations and tax offices will be left in the hinterlands. A friend of mine who lives in the suburbs of Saitama Prefecture told me how inconvenient postal services were getting as the organization consolidates itself:

When a package requires a personal stamp upon delivery and that person is not home, the postal worker will return the package to the post office and leave a note for the person telling him where his package is. In the past, you could go to the nearest post office with your stamp and retrieve your package. But these days, the package is returned to a post office in the next town, so there's no easy way to get it. I have to take the train two stops to get to the post office that has my packages. I waste half a day just getting my mail!

Readers Share Their Postal Nightmares

I write a new article for my website every day, and I get a lot of feedback from readers. I'd like to introduce a few of the many letters I received about privatizing the postal system.

Dear Mr. Morita,

The Koizumi cabinet was fond of lying about how much more convenient and improved the postal service was becoming, and yet, one year before postal privatization officially began, look at the mess the post office is in already.

"Reorganization" has a positive ring to it, but the reorganization of postal operations means that of the 49,696 branches throughout Japan, as many as 1,048 will offer only basic customer services, which means no collections and no deliveries. Many of the 167 branches in the Chugoku region and 160 branches on Hokkaido that were targeted for this reorganization have already been changed over, and all of them should be converted into customer-service entities by the end of the year. There are several branches in Tokyo slated for reorganization, too.

The government says the level of service won't drop, but I think the biggest difference will be that in the past, the staff could also handle our savings deposits and insurance, but now the "delivery specialists" will only handle deliveries.

On the face of it, slimming down postal collection services sounds good, but it means that in towns and villages where the mail was delivered at least three times a day, it will be delivered just twice. The early morning delivery will be cancelled. That means the packages and mail people bring to the post office in the evening will sit around until the following afternoon before being sent out. How is that not a reduction in service levels? This reform has already been put in place in the Tama area of Tokyo.

If you needed a savings card reissued, it used to be free, but from September 2006, it costs one thousand yen. Many other services that used to be free cost something today. How can the elimination of free services not be seen as a reduction in service levels?

International remittances used to have fees starting from five hundred yen and going up depending on the amount of money you were wiring. Now it has jumped to ¥2,500. Many other fees have risen as well.

The Japan Post Group has also explained the removal of many ATMs because they weren't profitable. The Koizumi cabinet went to the Diet and promised us that postal privatization wouldn't result in worse service. It would be "more convenient," they said. To make sure they keep their promise, they need to return to the Diet, take some responsibility and discuss what needs to be done to live up to their words.

If they don't do this, the people who supported privatization are going to realize that they've been hoodwinked by their own government.

Here are the comments of someone who works for the post office:

Dear Mr. Morita,

I want the people of Japan to realize what is going on in the post office lately.

1. Mail pickups: Because local branches are closing, people have to drive fifteen to twenty minutes to the next town to get their mail.
2. Mail drop-offs: You used to drop off your mail at a nearby postbox, but those are disappearing, and people have to travel farther to drop off their mail.
3. ATMs. The latest models won't accept coins. That means you can't pay your bills in cash. You have to either use your bank book or pay by card at the appropriate window.
4. Although it has yet to be decided, fees on other services are expected to rise and the burden is going to be more squarely on the backs of the customers from now on.

Is this what the people expected when they heard the talk of "privatization"? There is no sense in dragging out the irresponsible Junichiro Koizumi and **Heizo Takenaka** [the former minister of state for the privatization of postal services] and rebuking them at this point, but in the future, the people are going to realize that they've been ripped off.

Koubou Inamura is a friend I hold in very high esteem. He is also a guest professor at the graduate school in Chuo University and a former director of Japan's postal service. He wrote the following letter to me about Japan's post offices, especially its so-called convenient post offices, which could be found throughout Japan and were run by individuals, unions or other organizations.

Dear Morita-san,

The so-called *tokutei,* or specific, post offices with postmasters and a strong organization behind them are well known, but the smaller post offices, known as *kan-i,* or "convenient," post offices, are often in out-of-the-way villages, so they don't attract much attention. Today those **kan-i post offices** are in a calamitous state.

There once were 4,108 *kan-i* post offices, but their numbers have been in steady decline. This year alone [2007] about 280 were forced into temporary closure. Once the postal service inaugurated the plan, the pace of closures has rapidly increased.

While it was the rare post office that was managed by a fishery co-op or some such group, many were run by individuals who made their income off of service charges. They would piece together their income through the ¥130,000 in basic monthly service fees and other extra charges. Put all the charges together, and these small-town post managers made about four million yen or less a year—or at least about 70% of them did.

There were some outlets that made as much as ten million yen a year, but they were very few and tended to be inside department stores in big cities ... But generally, *kan-i* post offices brought quite meager income to their managers. The overall average ends up being less than three million yen a year.

Around 80% of the service fees came from people using their savings accounts. The post office's official stance has been to stop encouraging fixed deposits, which has led to fewer people using this savings tool, which in turn means smaller incomes for the postmasters of these smaller post offices. The average age of these postmasters is fifty-seven and trending upward. It's clear that the people who run these post offices are doing so out of a sense of mission to keep the regional economies afloat, because they can't survive on that type of income.

At the bigger post offices, there were reported to be from 2,300 to 2,400 postmasters ready to retire in spring 2007, compared with the usual seven hundred to eight hundred retirees. This is abnormally high, and it is happening alongside the shuttering of the *kan-i* post offices.

On October 25, 2006, Japan Post President Ikuta announced at a press conference that the agency had expenditures of three billion yen, which comes out to an increase of about ¥65,000 per post office per month. When the mass media reported this news, they framed it as a heroic tale of an agency trying to support its rural network. But the truth is that the media glossed over the real story of how smaller branches were getting bullied and eventually failing ever since the post office became the Japan Post [a name it held as its services were consolidated from 2003 to 2007].

What do the people in charge, the new managing class of the Japan Postal Agency, have in store for the horizontally structured *kan-i* post offices, which serve Japan's outlying areas and create a national network? It is not yet clear. I've heard that some want to put forth a test that the postmasters would have to pass to continue handling savings accounts and insurance. This was the talk as the dawn of privatization approached in 2007. It's as if they're looking for ways to push the elderly postmasters out of their jobs.

Without that national network of smaller post offices, the provinces will suffer. To save this network from the onslaught of market ideology and the servile bureaucrats, politicians most either rethink or turn back the postal privatization process.

What follows is an excerpt of a speech by a former People's New Party lower house representative Kouki Kobayashi. Kobayashi gave the speech on December 6, 2006, to a packed house at the Sunshine City Prince Hotel in Tokyo as part of the Johoku Economists' Gathering, as the event was billed. Morita also spoke to the crowd, which he estimated as five hundred or so, many of whom stood throughout. Kobayashi's speech was entitled, "Japan, Is This What We Truly Want?"

The September 11, 2005, elections left an ugly mark of historic proportions on Japan's constitutional government. When a bill passes the lower house but is rejected by the upper house, the expected route is for both house assemblies to discuss the bill. That process was denied and the lower house was dissolved. The party president used his political authority to silence any alternative views within the party, and party members who opposed the dissolution were effectively banished. What was left were assassin lawmakers, who hadn't really studied the bill, purging the party of dissent. It was not an election up to the standards of a country that likes to call itself an advanced democracy. But in the face of this, the major newspapers and TV networks accentuated the problem by trumpeting the election as a big victory for Koizumi.

The postal privatization law has its roots in a 2004 summit between US President Bush and Koizumi. Bush requested the privatization, and Koizumi agreed. But for some reason, the government and the mass media haven't told the Japanese people this. The very law itself was tailored to the demands of the Americans; Heizo Takenaka, then minister of state for the privatization of postal services, even said in his Diet testimony that he had seventeen meetings with American officials to discuss the bill. This is not a treaty, and yet they consulted a foreign country! Those within the Liberal Democratic Party who argued that outside pressure should be rejected were ignored, and the deliberative process that is supposed to be part of passing a bill was very abnormal. And yet, the mass media did not cover this story.

Furthermore, every year the American government brings the Japanese government a report detailing its requests for Japanese reforms, saying it is only trying to help Japan realize a profit ... But the Japanese government has not told its citizenry about the existence of this report.

In the end, as media around the world reported, the privatization bills were passed in Japan, and Wall Street couldn't have been happier. This was Japan's financial war; this was a fight to ensure continued American prosperity by putting Japan's financial assets under the American financial umbrella.

The structural reforms orchestrated by Koizumi and Takenaka, seemingly designed to respond to the early stages of bad loans by allowing foreign capital to buy up land and assets, were nothing more than a restructuring of Japan to fulfill American demands.

American life insurance companies were pushing hard for Japan's postal privatization. [The Japanese postal system was the largest of its kind in the world. It was also one of the world's largest financial institutions, providing savings accounts and selling life insurance.] They appealed to President Bush in a bid to abolish the convenient life insurance system in Japan through "postal privatization." That's the simple story. In other words, this privatization wasn't, as Koizumi was fond of saying, for the Japanese people; it was for the foreign capital that runs American life insurance corporations. The Japanese people were fooled like never before. Even postal operations are being privatized despite the US having a public postal system, and Japan's postal system, once praised for being the best in the world, is succumbing to the inevitable, caving in as post offices close across the country.

The mass media has never picked up on this story. Instead they continue their praise of Koizumi and Takenaka. Perhaps the large TV networks and newspapers don't want to offend one of their big sponsors, the American insurance industry. Many in the Japanese intelligentsia think the media is censoring itself.

Japanese people, let me ask you something: in the last decade, have you seen your income go up? You are some of the most diligent workers in the world who have set an overwhelmingly high standard with technology. Why aren't you getting paid more?

Next door in China, economic growth for the last ten years has continued at nearly 10%. Europe and the US and other advanced nations have reached 4–5%. But our country's economic stagnation continues. We work and work and work, but then the invisible hand of foreign capitalists comes and deftly takes your money away. Our country works for American prosperity, while the average Japanese citizen works with all his or her might just to keep up. Look at the increasing wealth gap in Japan and you'll understand how it works: the politicians and economists who kiss up to America have a high place in society and an equally high income.

While Japan should be one of the most abundant countries in the world, instead we are abolishing fixed-rate income tax reductions, the elderly are paying more for medical treatment and we're all bearing more of a burden for insurance. There's even talk that the consumption tax is going to go up. As I talk to you about this, perhaps many of you are realizing for the first time that postal privatization in our country is not being done for us. Many of our citizens have been hoodwinked by the government and the media. We have to realize that we are in the middle of some intense international competition. We must get ahold of ourselves and build an independent nation.

To build a politics that is of the Japanese people, by the Japanese people and for the Japanese people, you must rise to action.

Japan, open your eyes!

CHAPTER 14

AMERICA'S NEXT TARGET
JAPAN'S ME

J APAN'S MEDICAL SYSTEM IS FACING A SERIOUS DILEMMA. It's becoming clear that Koizumi's medical reforms are destroying the country's health system. The mass media doesn't even report this, but the American government has made it plain from before in its annual reform recommendations that it wants medical reform to follow postal privatization in Japan.

The Japanese government has started to reform the medical system because American medical organizations have been applying pressure on Japan through the US government to loosen restrictions on treatment and substantially change the way the Japanese get their health care. The US also wants Japan to dismantle its health insurance system and open everything up to American firms.

On June 14, 2006, the Koizumi administration followed up on the previous year's postal privatization movement with Japan's worst law of the twenty-first century, the **Medical System Reform Law**. The bill was filled with so many things that should have made it impossible to get through the Diet, but the ruling coalition of the Liberal Democratic Party and New Komeito bulldozed it through.

Japan's medical system is supported by a health-insurance plan that caters to the country's large middle class, a product of decades of strong economic growth. Where is the urge to change this system coming from? It's not coming from within Japan. Koizumi's government

CAL SYSTEM

felt compelled to "reform" (more like "ruin") Japan's medical system because of strong pressure from the American government.

The reality is that the Americans are about to take over Japan's health-care system. Koizumi, our former premier, did the bidding of the Americans and led Japan's medical system down the road to ruin. Koizumi's reforms—his American revolution directed by the American government—have brought Japan's medical system to the point where it will be picked over by insatiable American investors. For example, there is a movement now for something called "mixed examinations," which is really a euphemism for pushing low-income people aside. In the first book of my trilogy on Japan's subordination to the US, which I co-authored with Takehiko Soejima (*Amerika Ni Kuitsukusareru Nihon* [*A Japan Served up for American Consumption*], Nihon Bungeisha, 2006), Soejima uncovered this plan to deliver two-tiered health care under the "mixed examinations" system.

This system aims to introduce another layer of health examinations for the rich. The system is being pushed by American insurance and pharmaceutical companies so that they can get a foothold in the Japanese medical-examination sector.

Less Money Made in Medical Exams Means Less Effort Managing Hospitals

Japan has a doctor shortage. Hospital administration is also suffering. Some hospitals are facing a crisis as costs for medical treatment go up and the number of patients drops. One more reason for this crisis is that the Finance Ministry's power within the government has grown, and as it controls more of the budget, it is furthering a government aim to force some hospitals out of business.

The government, led by the Health Ministry, believes that hospital administration should be Americanized, and if a hospital isn't managed correctly, it should be shut down. The shuttered hospitals are then picked over by American **vulture-capital funds**.

An era of medical malaise has begun in Japan. The age when anyone — rich or poor — could be treated is almost over.

An excellent pamphlet on this issue, called "The Disappearance of Medical Treatment; The Disappearance of Life," was published by Hodanren, a national federation of medical insurance groups. The subtitle of the pamphlet is, "How did we end up with a doctor shortage and the emergence of patients with nowhere to go for treatment?"

According to the group, Japan had 6,398 functioning obstetric clinics or hospitals in 2002. By 2005, more than half of those clinics and hospitals were gone and only 3,063 remained (clinics plunged from 4,648 to 1,783, while hospitals dropped from 1,750 to 1,280).

The same trend is seen in pediatrics: In 1994, there were 3,938 hospitals offering pediatric services; in 2004, there were 3,281. Japan's medical infrastructure is in rapid decline.

Here are some excerpts from the pamphlet:

The reason for the shortage of doctors in universities and hospitals is first and foremost because the absolute number of doctors in Japan is too low. This is a result of long-term government policy on training medical professionals. In 2004, Japan had about two doctors for every one thousand people. According to the Organisation for Economic Co-operation and Development [OECD], that placed Japan at twenty-seventh in a survey of thirty countries.

The second reason for the shortage is that there is no care taken to cover costs in Japan. There is a fundamental problem with a country that won't sufficiently fund its own medical care. Also, the government and the Health Ministry aren't doing anything to stem the shortage of doctors. The ministry claims there is no shortage of doctors, but that the problem lies in the distribution of medical care. This is horrible sophistry. It's a random argument by the bureaucrats.

Behind this bureaucratic sophistry is the real reason for the collapse of Japan's medical system: American demands and cost controls put on medical spending by the Japanese government. The government is trying to get out of the medical-treatment business when it should be making health care a top priority. Operating a medical-treatment system is one of the most important jobs of government. Ever since Koizumi became prime minister, the government has been trying to renege on its responsibility to provide that care.

It makes me want to ask the politicians in the LDP and New Komeito what they've done with their humanity. The ruling coalition is developing its own brand of anti-human governance.

In the US, 17–18% of the people have no insurance and can't get treated for ailments. There's no space in American hospitals for the poor. They have to wait until they get really ill, then get carted to the emergency room in an ambulance. As a result, most people arrive well past the point where treatment can help. "If they had just arrived a little earlier, we could have helped" — America is filled with such cases.

There are also a lot of cases where an amputation occurs because the person comes in too late for help and medical treatment can't save the limb. More and more people suffer handicaps because of serious illness or injury that goes untreated for too long. This is the path America has been headed down, but recently the country has shown the will to change this. Many of the presidential candidates in the early part of the campaign for the 2008 election made some sort of promise about getting everyone covered for medical treatment. And Hillary Clinton has promised to make sure every American citizen has some sort of health insurance. With Clinton and Barack Obama competing for the Democratic nomination, if either one were to become president, the US medical system would take a turn for the better. The country is turning away from the Bush doctrine and beginning to take responsibility for its health care and welfare.

Japan alone is unthinkingly running toward these extremes, Bush-inspired, free-market policies. We're in danger of jumping onto this Bush doctrine just as the Americans are distancing themselves from their president. We get into the Bush rocket, somebody ignites it, we set off all by ourselves for space and wander around aimlessly. That's the danger we face.

For example, in the field of dentistry, pay has been kept low for many years. Insurance covers some treatments but none that employ the latest technology. In the pamphlet I mentioned earlier, "The Disappearance of Medical Treatment; The Disappearance of Life," dentists are quoted as saying, "I used to be able to get by on insurance, but I've had all that I can take," and "I can't continue under the current insurance setup."

Since the Japanese government is reluctant to spend on medical care, Japanese medical expenditures rank last among the seven leading industrialized countries and twenty-seventh of thirty industrialized countries, according to the OECD. Japan also had the highest co-payments of the countries surveyed.

The government has discarded the idea of running a welfare state and has destroyed the medical system. But is it really OK for the government to just turn its back on the responsibility to provide health care? Or should medical care be the very thing government provides? The Japanese people are struggling with this fundamental question right now.

The Japanese government has support for its medical policies from the American government. The Americans want to remake Japan's economy and see how much they can profit from it.

The administrations of former premiers Koizumi and Abe listened to whatever the Americans requested and turned the Japanese medical system over to the Americans' huge monopolistic capital funds to feast on. It's a treasonous policy, and we must not forgive them for it. As the next election season approaches, the Japanese people must see clearly which politicians want to destroy the medical system and which want to help it, then vote appropriately. If we do this, we can save our health-care system.

Koizumi's reforms tried to force Japan's medical and welfare system into the American capitalist model, and this has resulted in the system's collapse. Health care and welfare don't mix well with free-market principles. Medical care should be the responsibility of the government. The Japanese government should pay less attention to the American military and more to the health of its own people.

CHAPTER 15

AGRICULTURAL REFORMS PUSH SMALL SCALE

A GRICULTURAL REFORMS PASSED DURING THE KOIZUMI administration were continued in subsequent administrations. The reform law that is causing all the problems raises the following issues:

1. It sets a goal for agricultural exports to leap to one trillion yen in 2013. They were worth ¥330 billion in 2005.

2. The bill calls for aggressive farming. Koizumi was the advocate for this back in June 2006, when the bill was passed into law. The law focuses most of the subsidies on large-scale farms and agricultural organizations. The law is meant to promote large-scale farming and make Japan's agricultural sector more efficient. Abe continued down this path, and the next step is supposed to be the elimination or reduction of tariffs.

3. People have questioned where this bill leaves the small-scale farmer and whether it will increase unemployment in the rural areas.

This aggressive stance on farming, which Koizumi pushed during his term, tries to turn Japan's agricultural sector into a flawless capitalist machine. The attempt is fundamentally flawed.

Farming is not something that typically lends itself to the strictures of capitalism. The production of food is something basic and

MERS TO THE BRINK

essential for humans. If we follow the current trends, we see that people are becoming more aware of the dangers of tainted food. An agricultural policy to match the times should stress a stable supply and more hands-on farming. There should be a mix of large-, medium- and small-scale farms working together. And there should be room for even the family farmers.

There are a multitude of things to consider when thinking about farm management. Japan's agricultural sector is made up of farms of many shapes and sizes. It's a huge mistake to think that you can just take a smaller-scale farm that is less efficient and merge it together with larger ones. The agricultural policies of recent political leaders make me think of Stalin's farm policies in the 1920s and 30s. That's how bad they are.

We can't allow ourselves to forget the truth about Japanese farming. We must acknowledge that mega-farms have been destroying agricultural operations which used to excel in Japan. We need to put on the brakes before Japanese agriculture declines further.

The driving force behind Japan's healthy approach to agriculture has been the small-scale farm. Today, the government pressures farm managers to do its bidding and dangles subsidies in front of small farms if they agree to consolidate with others. Trying to revive Japanese agriculture in this way is akin to climbing a tree in search of fish.

Withdrawal of Funds from Rural Areas Puts Smallest Farms at Risk

Japanese agriculture is in dire straits. One example of the problems farms face is the aggressive withdrawal of money from part-time farms. Since fiscal 2007, "reforms" were put in place to distribute subsidies to farmers who cultivate at least a certain minimum area of land. This has caused some of the smaller and midsize farms to try to get back the land they lent to big corporations, causing disputes over land. The government wants to reduce the number of small or part-time farms from two million to forty thousand.

This is a huge mistake. The smallest farms are necessary for Japan's agricultural community to thrive because they protect Japanese agricultural traditions.

In February 2007, NHK aired a special on the farm reforms that featured a small-scale farmer fighting off poverty. The screen filled up with the beautiful scenery around Tanada, a rural enclave in the Chusankan area of Shikoku island. Because government subsidies to Tanada had been discontinued, the area was going through construction known rather ominously as the "narrow land correction."

This topographically diverse area was being flattened out into a plain in a bid to expand farmland and thus once again become eligible for subsidies.

But the local farmers were despondent because the leveling of their peaks and valleys would eliminate the different qualities of Tanada rice, which tastes different depending on the elevation of the crops. This is the type of stupidity propagated by Koizumi and Abe through their agricultural reforms.

Today's capitalistic systems came about as the factory took center stage in developed economies. Farming is fundamentally different from industry; for one, agriculture is not very productive when measured by current industrial standards. The Japanese can't harvest their rice crops two or three times a year. Organic farming needs to obey the rules of nature.

Of course, industrialized farming, like any industry, can raise production through artificial means. But the sort of production spoofed in Charlie Chaplin's *Modern Times* can't be replicated in farming. Capitalistic reforms of farming are replete with problems. The basic characteristic of agriculture is that the farmer follows the annual cycle. Nature is the ultimate authority in farming.

The American experience with large-scale farming has exposed many problems. There are few family farms left, and yet it is the small-scale farm that makes the best product. It is a huge mistake to force these small-scale farms into extinction.

The Opposition's Stance

Japan ranks quite low when it comes to agricultural self-sufficiency. While countries across the globe work to raise their ability to feed their own populations, the Japanese government treats the whole issue with a lack of enthusiasm. Japan's current self-sufficiency rate is 40%, which means the country makes 40% of the food necessary to feed the Japanese population. The government has neglected efforts to improve this low rate.

Other industrialized countries are far ahead of Japan: The US has a self-sufficiency rate of 127%; France is at 136%; Germany is 97% self-sufficient; and the UK is at 71%. The Japanese government only has eyes for the US, and as long as the Japanese government's utmost concern is satisfying the desires of the Americans, Japan's self-sufficiency rate won't improve.

Opposition Democratic Party of Japan leader Ichiro Ozawa has been taking a different stance on farm reforms during campaigns: "First, our food supply should be made safe and stable." He advocates less reliance on imports and the establishment of true self-sufficiency. He criticized the blind pursuit of efficiency by the Liberal Democratic Party leaders because it leads to the neglect of the small farm. Instead, Japan needs a policy that allows small-scale farmers to make a living and lets both the old and the young take part. To support and expand Japanese agricultural production, Ozawa is pledging to institute a subsidy that would pay farmers the difference between their production cost to grow basic agricultural products and the price those products get in the open market. On this issue, the DPJ's policies are far ahead of the ruling coalition.

If the Japanese government subsidizes the income of the nation's farmers, Japan's agricultural sector will make a comeback.

CHAPTER 16

PATRIOTISM & US INFLUENCE I

O N NOVEMBER 15, 2006, THE MEMBERS OF FOUR OPPOSITION parties — the Democratic Party of Japan, the Japanese Communist Party, the Social Democratic Party and the People's New Party — boycotted a Diet committee vote on a proposal for basic educational reform, saying deliberations had not been completed. In the opposition's absence, the ruling Liberal Democratic Party and New Komeito decided on their own what should be at the core of Japan's educational system.

For those two parties to decide on a law that restricts education well into the future is the height of arrogance. It's something I don't think we should forgive.

The government wanted to use the **Educational Reform Bill** to instill the education system with a heightened spirit of fairness, morality, respect for Japan's traditions and culture, the virtues of the samurai and a love for the country. There was also a sentence in the bill about patriotic training: "Foster the virtues of love and respect for the samurai and our country's traditions and culture."

While these are important qualities to instill in students, I don't think they need to be emphasized in law. I worry that Japan's future will include more rules and regulations enforcing patriotic education.

HE CLASSROOM

Educational Reform from the Occupation to Today

Japanese education faces another issue: the many reforms pushed through by former Prime Minister Koizumi are beginning to take effect. These reforms are bound to have a very negative effect on the nation's education system.

Koizumi went down the list of reform requests the Americans submit each year and made sure to enact measures Americans could profit by in the areas of postal service, medicine and agriculture. But the US has one more goal for reform: Japanese education. The Americans come in and break the education system, then support a reformed version that investors can pick over for profits. Under the name of "reform," Japan is turning its educational system into a business venture for American investors. Why was then Prime Minister Abe so bent on complicating the matter of educational reforms? To understand, we need to have a good grasp of the history of American influence in Japan's educational system, which begins during the postwar Occupation.

On August 30, 1945, General Douglas MacArthur touched down at Atsugi Naval Base. At the time I was a junior high school student in the nearby town of Odawara, so I remember his arrival well. On

September 2, Foreign Minister Mamoru Shigemitsu signed the instruments of surrender aboard the USS Missouri. It was an unconditional surrender placing Japan under the control of the **General Headquarters (GHQ)**.

The GHQ enacted all sorts of measures when it was in control of Japan. It dismantled the Japanese army, recognized human rights, instituted women's suffrage, democratized the education system and encouraged workers' unions to form. A little less than a year and three months after the war ended, on Novemver 3, 1946, Japan's new Constitution was announced. The Constitution was officially put into effect on May 3, 1947.

The basic principles espoused by Japan's Constitution include fundamental human rights, sovereignty of the people and pacifism. Because Japan was under the control of the GHQ at the time, it was as if the Western current of democracy that had been building since the Renaissance had rushed into conquered Japan, and the Constitution stipulated this fact. The Fundamental Law of Education was enacted with the spirit of the Japanese Constitution in mind.

The law's first article states:

> Education shall aim at the full development of personality, striving for the rearing of the people, sound in mind and body, who shall love truth and justice, esteem individual value, respect labor and have a deep sense of responsibility, and be imbued with the independent spirit, as builders of a peaceful state and society.

Many Japanese people supported the philosophy of the Fundamental Law of Education and welcomed its enactment.

As a result of this Western-style democracy taking root in Japan, teachers' organizations rapidly strengthened. One such group was the Japan Teachers Union. The teachers union grew in numbers and strength along with the broader union movement in Japan.

At the same time, the postwar political arena began with three main parties: the **Liberal Party** and the **Democratic Party**, which were both conservative, and the **Socialist Party**, which stood for democratization of society. The Liberals and Democrats merged in 1955 to form the Liberal Democratic Party. Since that point, the newly merged conservative parties were intent on finding ways to weaken the teachers union, which was aligned with the Socialists.

In postwar Japan, positions on the various boards of education were decided through elections. But then the LDP and some Education Ministry bureaucrats changed the process from elections to appointments in a bid to remove the influence of the union. The system of appointing board of education members has been tweaked many times over the years and is still a hot topic—it was the main focus of three educational reform bills submitted during Abe's tenure.

The conservatives have consistently tried to go through the boards of education to bring more patriotic regulation into the education system.

Until about the middle of the 1960s, Japan's university system and educational institutions maintained for the most part their autonomy and an open curriculum. However the student protest movement in the latter half of the 1960s led to the collapse of autonomy and open curricula on Japan's campuses by the first part of the 1970s. The postwar left-wing movement was choked off right here. The student protest movement and progressive scholars butted heads and both fell to the ground.

This is the larger meaning of the student protest movements. They put an end to the postwar left-wing movement, allowing the conservatives to take the lead in setting the education agenda. From that point on, the LDP's conservative wing took control and infused Japanese education with a right-wing ideology.

Reviving Patriotism by Revising the Education Law

The phrase "pro-American conservative" has entered the Japanese lexicon recently. You'll find this type ensconced in Japan's universities. While the progressive academics were chased away from the lectern, the pro-American conservative instructors have taken over Japan's higher education. Because of this, there are more and more students stuck in conservative ways these days. They go onto careers in the government, the central bank, large financial institutions and the media; these students then further the current right-leaning tendency in government, industry and communications. The LDP uses subsidies to make sure there isn't a gap in salaries and amenities between private and public universities. This funding keeps the private universities under the control of former Education Ministry officials and the education "specialists" in the LDP, and creates a structure where the LDP and the ministry are as one in their support of education.

In the provinces, the boards of education dominated by conservatives are run like exclusive monopolies. As time elapsed, we were brought to the point where former Prime Minister Abe could bring out his educational reform plan. The LDP has complained that the Fundamental Law of Education doesn't allow for Japanese patriotism; this is the reason they give for the reforms. Their coalition partner New Komeito provides an echo chamber for the LDP's argument.

The GHQ abolished imperial decrees on education and denounced a war that was fought under the ideals of "loyalty and patriotism." Obviously, the sort of patriotic education Japan had before the war was rejected. Later on, the LDP worked hard to revive this very sort of patriotic education and tried to get the teachers union and ideologically inclined cultural figures to support the idea. This is how the idea of the Educational Reform Bill was born.

However, the bill didn't have a chance of passing the Diet until New Komeito, the LDP's ruling coalition partner, agreed to support it. New Komeito made the LDP's longtime dream a reality.

Koizumi presented the bill to the Diet, but this really wasn't Koizumi's area of interest.

Then Abe came along. Constitutional revision and educational reform were the centerpieces of "Abe politics." He quickly pushed the bills toward passage.

Abe used the issues of constitutional reform and education as controversial tools to garner support for his government. But this approach tends to leave unhealed wounds. An issue as important as the basic thrust of Japanese education should have been debated thoroughly, but in the end, the LDP and New Komeito rammed the bill through both houses and decided the matter on their own.

The two parties went too far. A day of reckoning will come for the LDP and New Komeito. If another party comes to power, it may undo these reforms. But we'd be far from our goal of having a stable educational philosophy if the basic philosophy for the nation's education changes each time a new political party takes power. That's not education. At the very least, any sort of educational reform should be done in a nonpartisan fashion. Generally, the Abe educational reforms have to be seen as a huge failure. The issue should have been debated thoroughly in the Diet until at least 80–90% of the legislators agreed with the reforms presented to them.

The American Strategy: Don't Raise Elitists

To begin with, the boards of education operating during the Occupation adopted and spread evenly throughout Japan an educational system that was borrowed in part from the US.

The boards were established as the GHQ decentralized the provinces. To keep the prime minister from directly controlling these entities, the Education Ministry was weakened and board members were elected. But once the Occupation ended, the process was changed so that the chair of each board of education was hand-picked by the government and given more power.

The nation shouldn't control education. This was the basis of postwar educational thinking. I believe education should be privately conducted. When the **imperial university system** was reformed after the war, I believed that it should have been abolished. But that didn't happen. The **national university system** continued.

I believe that after the war, the Americans wanted to eliminate the elites from Japanese society. Before the war, the elite students would be educated in high schools and then progress into the imperial university system. At these old-style high schools, the education was quite specialized. The textbooks were originals for that school, and in some classes the students were expected to take notes and answer in a foreign language. Studying another language was required, and students were expected to excel in English, German or another language.

During the three years of high school, training in both the social and natural sciences helped cultivate a well-rounded, intelligent student body. They studied philosophy, literature and religion in a convivial yet hard-working atmosphere. Most of the students lived in dormitories. These high schools trained the students to cultivate a spirit of leadership.

This high school system, which cultivated young minds into elite thinkers, was a source of strength for Japan through the formative Meiji Era until the nation's defeat in World War II.

The GHQ wanted to do away with this system once and for all.

The typical view of prewar Japan's education system is that it was a single-minded, militaristic one that offered no freedom to students. The truth is not so simple. Although in the end, everything was destroyed under militarism, Japan's prewar education system was quite free.

The system was also very flexible. It was normal for a fifth grader who did well on the middle school entrance exam to jump ahead a grade. if you studied, you could excel. Middle school also had five grades, but in the fourth year, a student could try the high school entrance exam. Normal education finished after sixth grade, the last year of elementary school, and for students who weren't going on to middle school, there was a special two-year course they would take. Then they'd graduate and start working. If a student failed the middle-school exam, he or she could study in the special extended elementary school course for a year and try again. In fact, students could try the test again and again. That's how flexible the system was. The old-style high school provided students with three years of freedom. And the alternative private courses, which were the equivalent of high school, were also enveloped in an atmosphere of freedom.

The 6–3–3–4 Illness

The prewar educational system spanned seventeen years in a 6–5–3–3 configuration. After the war, this was changed to the American 6–3–3–4 structure. Losing a year of education was one thing, but the thing that really hurt was the compartmentalized approach to education that the Americans imported. This was all about the Americans keeping Japanese power tapped down.

When the Americans occupied Japan after the war, they wanted to be sure that the Japanese would not be able to wage war again; they figured that they should take away both the country's physical ability and its will to fight. To wage war successfully, a nation needs a high level of education, skill with technology and industrial prowess. The Americans saw these abilities in the Japanese as a threat—the potential for Japan to wage future wars—so the first order of the Occupation was to make sure that Japan didn't excel in these areas and that a future war begun by Japan would be a thorough impossibility. This is the basis behind the US Occupation of Japan.

The GHQ's first order of business was thorough inspections. On September 19, 1945, the GHQ unveiled its **Press Code**, which prohibited publication or broadcast of anything defending Japanese militarism or affirming prewar or wartime Japan, anything that supported warfare, criticized the Tokyo War Crimes Trials or the US military, and any report related to the atomic bombing and fire-bombing of Japan.

Jun Eto, a Japanese man of letters, wrote a book in 1989 entitled *Tozasareta Gengo Kuukan* (*Shutting Out the Space for Words*) that dealt with inspections by the US military during the Occupation. He relates how prepared and well executed these Occupation-era inspections were. This excellent book shines light on the period with an analysis backed up by original source material. Eto called the US inspections "a war of annihilation on Japanese thought and culture."

The postwar reforms instituted by US forces included women's suffrage, the right to form unions, abolition of the secret police, democratization of the economy and one more: control of the Japanese government by the GHQ.

This is how the postwar education system came to be. Progressives embraced the new emphasis on liberty and democracy, but there was little debate about the system's faults. The American system's merits include the popularization of education and the extension of mandatory education by one year. However, it was these positive aspects of the new system that raised doubts and discontent among conservatives. We've been fighting to shape this system ever since.

America Inc.: Turning Japanese Schools into Corporations

One piece of the Koizumi structural reform package—the designation of special districts where corporations could open schools—is quickly coming to a dead end.

Koizumi was in charge of the the Special Zones for Structural Reform, an effort to create special districts and begin reforms and deregulation in education, agriculture and social welfare that were supposed to fit each area's special characteristics. They were also supposed to enliven the regions and strengthen the local economies. This was the thought behind the law that was passed on December 18, 2002.

Before the law went into effect, only an educational organization could establish a private school in Japan. But since 2003, a corporation that worked within this special system could establish a school. As of this writing, Japan has six universities that are operated by corporations including LEC University, Digital Hollywood University and Business Breakthrough University. There are also thirteen high schools and one middle school run by corporations.

Recently, one of these corporate-run schools was found in an Education Ministry survey to have been breaking the rules; the ministry issued an advisory that the school must improve.

The problems of this corporate school are widespread: it's losing money; it was said to have far more registered students than actual students; the instructors lack leadership skills; the school library doesn't have many books—the list goes on and on.

The school didn't even have an independent building. Full-time university students took exams alongside prep-school students. And many of the university instructors doubled as prep-school instructors.

I don't believe the Japanese are going to warm up to this corporatization of the schools. Schools are things that really shouldn't be messed with too much. The system we have in place now for operating schools basically works. We have both private and public schools, and the current system allows us to see the strengths of both.

Schools need some financial devices to operate, but the government should help schools that fall on hard times. They could be run by alumni or parents with a vested interest in the school, for example. But there is something fundamentally wrong with turning schools into corporations and running them to make money. What happens to schools run like corporations? The CEO becomes the head of the school and appoints the dean. There would be no autonomy for the teachers.

Education and social welfare should not be run on competitive market principles. Education is an important asset to society. It should be given a tax status that allows it to welcome volunteers, freely accept contributions and makes it as easy as possible for the largest number of people to support it. And if that doesn't work, then the government should come to the rescue. Political parties and politicians should not interfere or use education for their own political ends. Education should be free to disengage from the political disputes of the day.

Japan as America's Triple-A Farm Team

Foreign-owned corporations are scouting the cream of the student crop in Japan these days. This is part of a US strategy to split Japan into two classes.

The best example of this strategy is found in professional baseball. The professional baseball world is clearly split into two. The best talent is paid big money to compete in Major League Baseball. Japan's professional league is quickly becoming the MLB's farm team.

When a player begins to excel, he becomes a free agent and heads to the US. Everybody agrees that it's a good thing.

NHK and the private TV networks air daily broadcasts on the achievements of Japanese players in the MLB. Meanwhile, Japan's pro leagues become farm teams of the American leagues.

Blame for this rampant Mammonism clearly lies with the mass media, especially the TV networks. Is it really necessary to broadcast from dawn to dusk the latest stock prices and exchange rates? I can't help but think that something is out of whack. Isn't this sort of information only used by a small group of people?

Kyoto University Professor Yoshihiko Yamamoto wrote a book in 2006 called *Uraretsuzukeru Nihon; Kaiasaru Amerika (The Continued Selling of Japan by America the Hunter)*. The subtitle of the book translates as "The US Reform Program for Japan and Our Fleeting Future." Here's one of the arguments presented in his book: "The US is demanding that the branches of foreign campuses opened in Japan be given the same privileges, including preferential tax treatment for students, as Japanese universities. If this is granted, Japan's higher education system will turn into a prep-school system for the US."

This is a serious problem. Too much of Japan is being turned into the Americans' bullpen, to further the baseball metaphor. We are splitting into two classes. The University of California system is the next one to eye a branch in Japan. The Japanese education system, which spans thousands of years and has cultivated the nation's unique culture and traditions, is being eaten alive by the three-hundred-year-old United States.

CHAPTER 17

CONSTITUTIONAL REFORMS
ON AN AMERI

I'D LIKE TO OFFER A BRIEF OVERVIEW OF THE ISSUE OF constitutional reform in postwar Japan.

On August 15, 1945, Japan unconditionally surrendered and ended its role in World War II. In the approximately six years and nine months between its surrender and the signing of the San Francisco Peace Treaty on April 28, 1952, Japan was controlled by the American-led Occupation forces. US General Douglas MacArthur was the supreme commander of these forces, and he oversaw the management of Japan from his General Headquarters (GHQ).

The GHQ's most important task was to make sure that Japan would not wage war again. It pushed through a series of deep reforms of Japanese society, abolishing the Imperial Army and the national police, dismantling the zaibatsu financial cliques and annulling the Imperial Constitution. This made way for the new Constitution, with its pledge of democracy, fundamental human rights and pacifism.

In 1954, Ichiro Hatoyama of the Democratic Party was ushered in as the new prime minister. Hatoyama had been an advocate of constitutional reform. In 1956, Hatoyama, who had presided over three successive cabinets, restored ties to the Soviet Union.

N TIMETABLE

Hatoyama eyed constitutional reform as a path to true independence. But he couldn't muster enough support during his term, meeting strong resistance from some, and thus his goal was never achieved. The interesting twist Hatoyama brought to the debate on the Constitution is that he was concerned first and foremost with Japanese independence from the US—that was the reason he wanted to revise the Constitution.

In 1955, Hatoyama's Democratic Party expanded its lead, but it still couldn't quite grab a simple majority. Around this time, the Liberal and Democratic parties came together to stabilize themselves. On November 15, 1955, the Liberal Democratic Party was born. The efforts of the Democrats to bring about constitutional reform now became a plan for the newly born LDP to carry out.

The GHQ had given Japan a peace Constitution in an effort to make sure that the nation could not wage war. Within Japan, there was a move to reform the Constitution to make it more reflective of an independent country.

About five years after World War II ended, on June 25, 1950, the Korean War officially began. MacArthur told then Prime Minister Shigeru Yoshida to form a National Police Reserve, and it was duly created in August of that year (the reserve was later turned into a security corps). Early the following year, MacArthur, reflecting the Cold War standoff that had altered the international scene by this time, began telling the Japanese government that it was time to rearm itself. Yoshida resisted these requests, but at the end of his fifth successive cabinet, in 1954, he established the **Self-Defense Forces** in order to "protect the peace, independence and safety of our country."

Forced to Sign: The 1951 Security Treaty

After the administrations of Hatoyama and Ishibashi had come and gone, Nobusuke Kishi became the premier and decided to examine the issue of constitutional reform. But the committee he formed to examine it decided that there was no need to pursue reforms. "The Self-Defense Forces do not violate the Constitution, thus there is no reason to pursue reforms," the committee said.

Kishi had skillfully used the committee to interpret the Self-Defense Forces as constitutional. He had convened the committee to push constitutional reforms, but when it ended up legitimizing the SDF through its constitutional interpretation, Kishi had achieved his goal and disbanded the committee.

While Kishi settled the constitutional revision issue in a muddled way, revisions of the 1951 US-Japan Mutual Security Treaty brought about a clear change in direction. Here Kishi abandoned any attempt of building an independent defense for Japan and set off down the road to American subjugation.

The original US-Japan Security Treaty of 1951 came out of the San Francisco Peace Treaty signing. The Americans put pressure on Prime Minister Yoshida to sign it. From that point on, Japan and the US were connected by the agreement, and the US military was able to establish military bases in the country.

The original treaty was extremely one-sided. Under international law, these types of treaties made when one country is occupying another become null and void when the other country achieves independence. Japan needed to annul this first treaty, but Kishi didn't do this. Instead, he continued this one-way treaty by agreeing to certain reforms.

There was opposition to this move among people who felt the treaty should be annulled under international law, but Kishi followed the American lead and agreed to reform and reaffirm the treaty, effectively giving new life to a treaty that then Prime Minister Yoshida was forced to sign. This is the real meaning behind the renewed security treaty between the US and Japan: the US military occupation of Japan would continue in perpetuity.

From Ron-Yasu to George-Junichiro

The cabinet after Kishi's was run by Hayato Ikeda, who was far more interested in rapid economic growth than constitutional revisions. Ikeda was a right-winger, but he was more focused on having Japan's economy grow peacefully. The following premier, Eisaku Sato, never pursued constitutional reforms.

In 1980, when Ronald Reagan won the US presidential election, the pacifist Zenko Suzuki was prime minister in Japan. Suzuki kept his distance from the new Republican leader. But then Yasuhiro Nakasone became the next prime minister, and the Ron-Yasu era was born. The quality of the US-Japan relationship changed during this time, with Japan marching further down the road of subordination to the US.

When the Republicans come to power in the US, the right-wing elements become strong in Japan. The Japan conservatives began putting more stress on constitutional and educational reforms.

From this point in the early 1980s, Japan began subjugating itself to Republican economic and political priorities. The Bush-Koizumi relationship was typical in this regard.

Current interpretation of the Constitution makes it impossible for the Self-Defense Forces to join in group exercises. There are two ways to change that. One is, raise the issue of constitutional reform. The other is to change the current interpretation of the clause in question.

However, "reforming" the Constitution by simply changing your interpretation is not fair and is not supported by the Japanese populace. One can't just spin a completely opposite meaning onto something without repercussions.

To reiterate: The American government wasn't very interested in pushing constitutional reform in Japan during much of the postwar era. But the Bush administration felt that taking a pro-reform stance was to its advantage. This change in the Americans' stance sparked a new surge of activity in Japan.

This is a dangerous road for the Japanese. These reforms are not about building an independent spirit in Japan. Instead, they are about aligning Japan behind the US global war strategy. This is the reality of the most recent round of constitutional debates. Japan should avoid reforming its Constitution just to fall further in line with US global policies.

Shinzo Abe began his short-lived premiership by boldly declaring that constitutional reform would be the centerpiece of his administration, following in the footsteps of his grandfather, Nobusuke Kishi. The unabashed failure of Abe's administration has quieted the reformers for the moment.

The Cure

THE SOURCE O

W AR, SURVIVAL-OF-THE-FITTEST ECONOMICS AND bureaucratic politics are at the root of the world's problems. The steps we need to take to begin to fix this mess are clear.

The US War Spreads Woe throughout the World

The Bush administration's war is the reason oil prices are skyrocketing, causing so many people to suffer. The war has also jeopardized the world's food supply. The US economic depression and subsequent confusion in economies throughout the world can also be pinned on Bush's war. The best way to reduce global suffering is to end this war and move toward peaceful solutions. But international opinion hasn't really galvanized around an "anti-war, pro-peace" message. Japan also seems scared of saying anything to the US government. The world should come together as one and tell the US to end this war—the US should admit its war is the source of the world's current problems.

UR SUFFERING

Politics Dominated by Bureaucrats Spread Woe throughout Japan

Lately, we've been hearing these phrases a lot: "the bureaucratic cabinet system" and the "Finance Ministry cabinet system." The country is going to realize soon that its political power is being controlled by elite bureaucrats in the central government and that the ruling coalition of the Liberal Democratic Party and New Komeito is being manipulated by these bureaucrats. People are waking up to the reality that the miserable situations with health care for the elderly as well as labor conditions for the young are rooted in initiatives taken by the bureaucrats. The plummeting approval ratings for the Fukuda cabinet are related to the unsettling realization among voters that the bureaucrats are running the government. This is also why the LDP's approval rating is so low. For the ruling coalition to improve its standing with voters, it must shake free of the bureaucratic grasp and return to parliamentary party politics.

Finding Common Ground

The leaders of the ruling and opposition parties should come together to figure out a path away from bureaucratic control and toward parliamentary democracy and party politics. They should share the task of moving from a bureaucratic cabinet system to a parliamentary cabinet system. As long as the ruling and opposition parties keep quibbling over trifles, it will be difficult to wrest the real political power from its current base in Tokyo's Kasumigaseki district, where the bureaucrats hold court. The Kasumigaseki elite will just rule in perpetuity. To strengthen party politics in Japan, both sides should come together and confer on the urgent issues facing the Japanese people today. They should search for areas to agree on and then set the stage for a national election. With the voters showing the way, our pressing need for vibrant national politics and a parliamentary cabinet system would be realized.

Needless Theories on Public Works Hold Japan Back

The Koizumi reforms were wrong when it came to weeding out "unnecessary" public works. The reason we've had a lot of water and gas accidents in Japan lately is that the infrastructure is getting old. Waiting for an accident before fixing things is a wasteful way to conduct one's business. But the government doesn't seem interested in recognizing this problem. It's a dishonest approach.

In the old days, you'd repair the pipes and that would be it, but now because of the reduction in funds for public works, the repairs aren't being made. We just wait for an accident, then patch things up. Essentially, we are wasting more money. Not to mention that the accidents disrupt our daily lives. This is the awful legacy of the Koizumi reforms.

Sewage pipes typically last forty to fifty years. The pipes carry microbes that create hydrogen sulfide, which erodes the iron frames and peels off the concrete over time. The road above can cave in and cause accidents. Before, these spots could be found ahead of time and fixed without incident. Accidents were easily prevented through this approach.

The same can be said about waterworks. In this case, the pipes and infrastructure typically last thirty years. Maintain the infrastructure with timely repairs, and there need not be any accidents. When there are accidents, repairs become very expensive.

Japan's Cutting Edge Sewage Technology

At the end of 2006, I conducted interviews at a water reproduction center in Tokyo's Shibaura neighborhood. Polluted water is cleaned up and returned to the rivers and ocean here. At one point, I drank some of the water as it was being sent back into the natural world. I felt fine. It seemed perfectly safe. The water made at this plant was also used to operate the building's toilets and refrigerators and helped reduce the heat-island phenomenon so prevalent in urban centers.

Improvement of urban environments leads to the improvement of the global environment. Solving the sewage problem is not just about figuring out how to live comfortably in an urban environment; it can also be very beneficial in our battle to protect the Earth.

Japan is a world leader in sewage technology. If this technology spread through China, for example, it would radically change that country's environment. And any improvement in China's environment would be a big boost for the Earth itself. If the technology could also be used in India, the global environment would improve by leaps and bounds. A few oil-producing countries are using this sort of technology, but if it could spread to other countries, the global climate would benefit greatly.

But this Japanese treasure may never be seen by the rest of the world because the companies that made it are on the verge of collapse. Essentially, the rapid decrease in public-works spending has been too fast for them to adjust. The life has been choked out of these small businesses as they try to operate within the confines of overly strict legislation. This amazing Japanese technology is facing extinction because of the utterly foolish Koizumi reforms.

Japan's sewage system is supported almost totally by small and midsize companies. The companies used to run research societies, but most of them were forced to close after a bid-rigging scandal. The societies were the subject of the bid-rigging investigation. Most of the companies have become quite passive because of the scandal. Some companies are facing the eleventh hour, possibly forced to pull away from sewage work.

A large company may be able to survive if it shuts down its sewage division, but that's not the case for these smaller sewage specialists. If they move away from their specialty, it is just a matter of time before they collapse.

Japan is a narrow country and it really needs to develop technology that will help it combat environmental problems. But the country's sewage industry is quickly falling apart. Just as it has a valuable contribution to make to the Earth's environment, the industry is dying out. Koizumi's trail of devastation even travels underground.

Following Gore

In his 2007 book, *An Inconvenient Truth*, the former US Vice President Al Gore gives us examples of the Earth's sickness and explains why it is on the brink of death. At the same time, he tells people what needs to be done to fix the problem.

So what should the Japanese government do?

I believe we shouldn't be cooperating with President Bush and his continuing war. Instead, we should change directions and begin down the path that Gore has described. We need a fundamental change in direction.

Bush has hardly even looked at the environmental problems we face. Once his Republican party was dealt a defeat in the 2006 midterm elections and the pressure from the Democrats rose, he made clear that he would begin to issue measures to combat climate change.

The environmental problems facing the Earth are very serious. The abnormal climate we have been experiencing lately is a byproduct of capitalism and industrialization. The polar ice caps are melting and ocean waters are rising.

Some countries are threatened by flooding. Japan already has the technology to become an environmentally advanced country; it can take polluted water and make it clean again. It has some of the best environmental technology on the globe. Japan should keep that technology alive for the sake of the whole world.

CHAPTER 19

FROM THE CLAS
TO AN ERA OF LE

E VERYTHING HAS ITS END. THE ERA OF US REPUBLICAN
Party rule is about to come to its end. The farcical Bush regime, with its extreme ideas about war and free-market
ideology, is months away from its end. Bush is about to retire. The
American people gave their verdict about Bush politics in the November 7, 2006, midterm elections, and since then the Bush ideology has been on rapid retreat.

The American midterm elections of 2006 marked a turning point
for world politics. I've been mentioning this in lectures since even
before the elections were held. On November 4, 2006, I delivered a
lecture in Osaka in which I made these main points:

> The Bush era is nearing its end. The American military is on its
> way out of Afghanistan and Iraq. The world is going through a

huge change, from war and toward peace. A change in values is under way.

The idea that Bush put forth was that the US military could use its superior strength to master the world. In the clash of civilizations, American society was supposed to muscle its way to world dominance, but his experiment ended in failure. The

F CIVILIZATIONS
ENED TENSIONS

American government is hated throughout the world. It is isolated and its politicians are racing to clean up all the mistakes.

Bush-style Republicans are in decline in the US, and the next leaders of American politics will be Democrats or Republicans who project a very different image from Bush, a more flexible diplomacy and a safer defense. Economic policies will also change. The old style of pressuring the rest of the world to play by American-style free market rules will begin to wane.

Because of this, the world is headed toward a more peaceful time. The conflict between Israel and Palestine won't be resolved soon, but because the giant US military presence will be in retreat, Middle Eastern disputes will become smaller. The world will transition from a clash of civilizations toward an era of lessened tensions.

Capitalism has two paths it can follow: Anglo-Saxon-style market economics or European-style modified capitalism, which combines a competitive marketplace within a social democratic system. The American choice of Anglo-Saxon market economics will no longer be the priority, and the European style will make a comeback, eventually replacing market fundamentalism. The social welfare policies that were neglected in Anglo-Saxon systems will make a comeback. Policies such as the ones the Republican Party put forth to accentuate the gap between rich and poor will be replaced by policies that try to close that gap.

In Japan, the practice of following the Republicans that was in vogue under Bush, Koizumi and Abe will fall out of favor, and politics that favor a modified form of economics will resurge. This is all connected to the coming transfer of political power.

When the two strains of capitalism existed in the Liberal Democratic Party, a change of power within the LDP was possible. However, five years and five months of Koizumi politics have destroyed the European strain within the LDP, turning the party into a one-lunged entity much like the Republican Party — unable to seek change from within.

After World War II, Japan lived under a US-led Occupation. Even after Japan achieved independence, it lived under the shadow of the American government. For the last six decades, Japanese politics have mirrored American swings from one party to the other. When the Americans swing toward the Democrats, a more centrist wing of the LDP rises; when the US swings toward the Republicans, the LDP's right wing gains power. The Democrats bring out the LDP's moderates; the Republicans bring out the LDP's right-wing hawks.

When Truman, a Democrat, was president, Japan had Shigeru Yoshida. When Eisenhower, a Republican, took over, Japan was led by Ichiro Hatoyama and Nobusuke Kishi. Hayato Ikeda rose to power with Kennedy, a Democrat. Nixon, a Republican, brought about Eisaku Sato. Carter, a Democrat, coincided with Masayoshi Ohira, and Reagan teamed with Yasuhiro Nakasone.

Clinton, another Democrat, served alongside **Tomiichi Murayama**, **Ryutaro Hashimoto** and **Keizo Obuchi**. And Bush, a Republican, was president while Junichiro Koizumi and Shinzo Abe ran Japan. That's sixty years of US-Japan relations.

There's a high probability that the opposition parties will gain a majority in Japan's upper-house election scheduled for the summer of 2007. [Editor's note: This turned out to be true as the opposition gained a majority in the upper-house vote, taking control of a house of the Diet for the first time in sixty years.] There's also a good chance that the lower-house election that must be held by September 11, 2009, will usher into power an alliance of opposition parties centered around the Democratic Party of Japan and usher out the LDP-New Komeito alliance.

The 2006 midterm elections in the US taking place two days from now will render Bush a lame duck. This will also mean that Bush's ability to sway Japan will be gone. Once a more Democratic-leaning administration is in place in the US, it will offer little resistance to the rise of the DPJ in Japan, making a political transition easier.

From 2007 to the summer of 2009, Japan's political landscape is likely to go through a major transformation. The economy will transition from the Anglo-Saxon, Republican model to a model more in line with Europe. Japan will be less subordinated to the US and more focused on balancing its relations with both the US and China.

For Japan, bringing political change through the voting booth is the first step to the country's revival. A new age of stable growth will follow.

Politicians bear a great deal of responsibility. How should a politician live? To answer that question, we should turn to *The Analects* of Confucius and his "nine cares of a gentleman." The gentleman that Confucius refers to could be interpreted today as someone who wields political power. Confucius offers nine lessons that any open-minded leader should heed. The interpretations presented here are mine alone, based on the ancient texts of Confucius.

FIRST, *when seeing, one should strive to see clearly.*

SECOND, *when listening to people, one should listen carefully and try to understand.*

THIRD, *one should wear a soft expression on his or her face.*

FOURTH, *one should conduct oneself in a respectable manner.*

FIFTH, *one should speak sincerely to others.*

SIXTH, *one should apply oneself diligently to new activities.*

SEVENTH, *when in doubt, one should ask questions and strive to understand.*

EIGHTH, *when angry, one should think of the consequences before acting rashly.*

NINTH, *when presented with an opportunity for personal gain, one should consider whether it is moral to take that opportunity.*

Confucius shows us the proper way of life for a leader. This teaching doesn't only apply to the leaders of the world; it is a teaching that the rest of us would also do well to follow. We would benefit especially by heeding the first, second and seventh cares when dealing with political issues today. Japanese politics are in danger of falling into a trap of historic proportions. Soon Japan will not be able to claim its sovereignty; it will be completely subordinated to the US.

The ruling parties, central bank, major newspapers and TV networks all hide this fact from the people. They will not tell the Japanese people the truth. Japan is heading down a dangerous road.

The Japanese people need to open their eyes. We can't entrust our future to a bunch of politicians who have lost their independent spirit due to years of being Uncle Sam's lackeys.

This is the time for the Japanese people to wake up to the new realities their country faces. In the end, the only ones who can save Japan are the Japanese themselves.

Epilogue

FROM MAYO

Minoru Morita dedicated much of his time in late January and early February 2008 to the re-election of Katsusuke Ihara, the mayor of Iwakuni City. Ihara's narrow loss, caused more by dirty tricks and strong-arm tactics than by any groundswell of support for his opponent, left a bitter taste (the story of the election is covered in chapter seven, "The Battle for Iwakuni City"). But Ihara is undaunted. As is so often the case with myopic policies that don't take into consideration the people affected by those policies, the heavy-handed push by the central government to have Iwakuni host more US military troops and equipment is breeding a generation of activists and politically aware citizens. And Ihara is bound to be at the front of the pack. Takehiko Kambayashi interviewed Ihara on May 26, 2008, to see how he was taking his election loss. This is what he had to say:

IN LATE DECEMBER 2007, I RESIGNED AS MAYOR BECAUSE THE city council rejected my budget proposal four times, which they should not have done. Two-thirds of the council's members are in favor of the US military realignment plans for Iwakuni.

They ignored the citizens of Iwakuni and tried to drag me down. I was not even able to discuss the budget with them. I kept insisting that the budget proposal was very important, but they would not listen. They were not opposed to the budget proposal itself, but

TO ACTIVIST

they turned it into a political tool. The way the city council acted was completely wrong, and the way the central government acted was irrational.

The government froze ¥3.5 billion [about thirty-four million dollars] earmarked for a new city hall and removed the city from the list of municipalities scheduled to receive base realignment subsidies in fiscal 2007. Meanwhile, my budget proposal was rejected by the council over and over again. I decided to resign in order to get it passed. I still had more than two years of my term left, but I turned to the voters. I told myself I must win.

The government gave us such a hard time. Yamaguchi Prefecture ... is a little lap-dog of a government, and its leaders continued to put pressure on us. Their pressure caused some trouble in various areas of the city government. This gradually began to worry city officials and residents. That's another reason I thought I should resign and run for mayor again. With the voters' mandate, I could renegotiate with the government. I knew this time I had to fight an uphill battle since more citizens felt uneasy about the city's situation; I also had to battle the central government and the prefectural government. But I still believed I was doing the right thing and thinking of our citizens.

Of course, I lost in the election on Feb. 10, 2008. Yet I don't think I really lost. The focal point of the election was supposed to be the US military's realignment plans in Iwakuni. But my opponent swept it under the rug. Instead, his campaign was based on fear-mongering, circulating groundless rumors about the city going bankrupt and city bus services stopping and the hospital leaving the city. The opposition camp also boldly claimed that the city could gain five to ten billion dollars from the central government if their candidate won. My opponent, current Mayor Yoshihiko Fukuda, made false promises such as free school lunches and free medical care for children. After he was sworn in as mayor, he said these were not really campaign pledges.

Moreover, the central and the prefectural governments exerted enormous pressure on Iwakuni citizens through various organizations and groups during the election campaign. Business leaders mobilized armies of their employees to help Fukuda win. On weekdays, workers wearing their factory uniforms came to the early voting in droves. Business leaders went all out [for Fukuda].

In the election—and it should be said that an election is the most important tool in a democracy—the voters' judgment was obstructed and they could not cast a ballot with a free mind. Unless such freedom is guaranteed, you cannot survey the will of the people. It was our own government that helped manipulate the ballot. I have to say that the foundation of Japan's democracy is not yet firm. As a result, what you have here is politics based on arm-twisting and deceit. I believe it is far from the sort of politics that benefits the voters.

I have campaigned and held office by seeking support from one citizen after another. I never relied on large organizations or interest groups. Our team consists of well-intentioned volunteers, so nobody in our camp thought of circulating false rumors even when our opponent was doing just that.

In retrospect, I have to admit some of our attempts to gain support from each and every voter were lax. We were deeply chagrined at the election loss because we believe the will of the voters was manipulated. Since the election drew a lot of attention from across the country, it was a must-win race, and I hoped our victory could help seize an opportunity to change politics in Japan. It was such an important race. That is why my loss disappointed my supporters. Certainly, I was also very disappointed.

Having said that, we are watching the city government. Now we have to face the politics of deception and lies. For example, Mayor Fukuda is now saying he will not accept the plan to realign US forces, yet behind the scenes he does just that in order to receive government subsidies. Nobody really believes he opposes the realignment.

We are concerned about Iwakuni's future and our children's future. We should not let this [US base expansion] happen. Recently, I have heard more people say that we should stand up once again. I also have received a lot of encouragement. We suffered a setback; however, I have a strong sense that we must continue activities to return our democracy to the voters.

My political ideal has always been to make Iwakuni a model of democracy. Building roads or facilities has never been my campaign pledge. I always say I want to change the political mechanics of government. So we have established a political group called Grass-Roots Network Iwakuni. This is not my support group; it's a political group based on a political ideal that all citizens can come together to change politics in Iwakuni and make the city a better place. Certainly, I am the one who directs the group, but I hope that it will become a kind of political party and someone will succeed me after I retire. We would like to conduct robust discussions, inviting citizens to join us and providing them with enough information so that they will not be deceived even in the midst of a dishonest election campaign with all of its inherent pressures and rumors.

Thus, we have started out once again to create a tenacious and tight-knit citizens network. In the first two months, our membership grew to three thousand, including people from other cities. We have begun to transmit our central message: "Our fight goes on." We will make our opinions heard while watching closely what is going on in the city government, especially since a lot of things are going on concerning the US military realignment plan. If necessary, we will issue a statement or file petitions or inquiries with the prefectural government or the city government. We may also carry out a signature-collection campaign, depending on the political situation.

We occasionally hold meetings and send out newsletters to provide citizens with information and strengthen the ties of our network. I have also launched a political institute called Somo Juku so that citizens could have a better understanding of politics and expand their own citizens networks. Through these activities, I would like to make people more aware of issues, nurture future politicians and support some politicians who have a similar political philosophy. In coming election campaigns, we will support candidates who share our political ideals. We will help them win and eventually change the city council and the current mayor.

On March 12, 2006, we had a nonbinding referendum on the US realignment plans to transfer an aircraft carrier from Atsugi to Iwakuni. The turnout stood at 58.68%, and 87% of the voters were opposed to the plan. I believe the referendum made many voters more aware of the issues. To resolve the issue of the realignment plans from the residents' standpoint, I believed at the time that we should change the political system and the way politics is conducted. Thus, as mayor, I found it absolutely necessary to hold a referendum and learn the will of the people. I also believe this sort of activity complements a parliamentary democracy. After the referendum, I realized that the vote increased the residents' awareness more than I had expected. Many people said to me, "Thank you for the opportunity" or "Thank you for asking my opinion." I have learned that they appreciate the referendum itself even more than its outcome.

Many voters told me that they did not feel they had a say in the city's policies and local base issues until the referendum changed the atmosphere.

To make the 2006 referendum successful, a number of civic groups sprang up in Iwakuni. Members of these groups were standing on the streets, calling for support and holding up their signs. After the referendum, these civic groups remain active even though the resolution was nonbinding.

We elect politicians. In many cases, however, they fall short of our expectations. So there is deep-rooted public mistrust of politics. It seems that many people think there is something fishy about politics. The image of politics in Japan is very bad. At a town meeting, one young man said, "We participate in politics through a filter called politicians. But they don't respond to our expectations, so I constantly feel very irritated. However, in a referendum, we make our own decision without such filters. This is a great opportunity." I found it interesting to hear him describe a politician as a "filter."

Many people don't think they can rely on the current political parties and politicians. Some voters complain that it's the same thing every time. I feel that today's politicians place priority on the benefit of a small number of people while downplaying the benefit of the public.

Since the political atmosphere in the US has changed a lot and we also are witnessing gradual change in Japanese politics, I don't think we should assume that the US military realignment plans will be carried out as planned. We should not give up hope.

Glossary

& Highly Idiosyncratic
Chin Music on Japanese Politics

CHIN MUSIC (chiefly US) 1. talk, chatter, gossip. 2. A pitch in base-ball that comes so close to the batter's chin that he can hear it go by; a warning or message pitch.

Chapter 2: THE UNBEARABLE BURDEN OF KOIZUMI'S REVOLUTION

SHINZO ABE — Served as Japan's ninetieth prime minister from September 26, 2006 to September 12, 2007. He resigned in dis-grace, exhausted and unpopular, after pledging to create more patriotic classrooms and to help the military expand. Abe was pursuing the same goals as his grandfather, Nobusuke Kishi, Ja-pan's prime minister from 1957 to 1960. *Chin Music:* Shinzo Abe's dad, Shintaro Abe, was Japan's foreign minister in the mid 1980s. He was on a short-list of potential prime ministers but then his career headed south when he was implicated in the Recruit stock scandal of 1988. Abe and many other politicians in the Liberal Democratic Party had been allowed to buy discounted shares of the publishing company Recruit Cosmos and had even been extended interest-free loans to buy the stock. For more on this sordid scandal, check out this comprehensive website: http://www.rcrinc.com/tanaka/ch5-3.html

JUNICHIRO KOIZUMI — Japan's eighty-ninth prime minister served from April 26, 2001 to September 26, 2006, when Shinzo Abe took over. Koizumi was wildly popular at first. He was seen as outspoken and daring, a maverick who broke from the drab Lib-eral Democratic Party mold. Even his hair—often referred to in the press as a "mane" or a "flowing mane"—set him apart. But his free-market, pro-US reform agenda was less popular, espe-cially his move to privatize the postal services and cut pension benefits. His legacy is much debated today. *Chin Music:* Koizumi divorced his first wife while she was pregnant with their third child. Koizumi took custody of the first two sons, and the boys have never seen or spoken to their mother since. The third son, who was born after the divorce, has never met his father.

KOIZUMI REVOLUTION — Refers to Junichiro Koizumi's series of free-market reforms and government restructuring of which the pinnacle was the privatization of Japan's postal system. Other reforms include cutting public-works spending, subsidies to provinces and pension benefits.

SHIZUKA KAMEI — A politician and founder of the People's New Party. Kamei was a member of the Liberal Democratic Party until 2005, when he formed his new party in protest over Junichiro Koizumi's postal privatization plans. *Chin Music:* Kamei is chairman of the Diet Members' League for the Abolition of the Death Penalty.

PEOPLES' NEW PARTY — Party founded by Shizuka Kamei in 2005 in protest over then Prime Minister Junichiro Koizumi's plans to privatize the post office.

TOKYO SHIMBUN — A daily newspaper distributed in the Tokyo area by parent Chunichi Shimbun Co. The paper has a morning and evening edition with a total circulation of about one million readers. *Chin Music:* Veteran journalist Sam Jameson relates this anecdote on the Foreign Correspondent Club in Japan's website: "In 1994, the *Tokyo Shimbun* prepared an advertising flier — apparently without the knowledge of the paper's editors – that was inserted into home-delivered copies of the *Asahi Shimbun* [see chapter eleven notes]. In it, the *Tokyo Shimbun* declared: 'All newspapers rely on the same news sources, so whatever newspaper you read contains virtually the same news as any other newspaper. Why not read the *Tokyo Shimbun* and save nearly ten thousand yen a year?'"

KOICHI KATO — A politician and lower house representative in the Liberal Democratic Party who has been seen throughout his career as a maverick—albeit a maverick from within the LDP. He had a hand in the rise of Junichiro Koizumi when he, Koizumi and Taku Yamasaki formed the YKK partnership to usher in a new generation of LDP leaders in the 1990s. But later Kato became a critic of Koizumi for the former prime minister's insistence on visiting the controversial Yasukuni Shrine, where war dead, including many war criminals, are memorialized. *Chin Music:* In August 2006, Kato made statements on TV criticizing Koizumi for his visits to Yasukuni Shrine on the anniversary of the end of the war. Later that day, Kato's house in Yamagata Prefecture was torched, allegedly by a right-wing group incensed over his criticisms of Koizumi. Kato's ninety-seven-year-old mother lived in the house but was not harmed.

LIBERAL DEMOCRATIC PARTY — The LDP has been the dominant party in Japanese politics ever since the Liberal Party and the Democratic Party merged in 1955. Despite its name, the LDP is a conservative, pro-US party. The LDP's power was largely unchecked for thirty-eight years, but in 1993, it lost its majority in the lower house of the Diet. An opposition coalition formed a government for a brief time. By 1996, however, the LDP was back in power. It held onto that power, including a resounding victory in September 2005 under the leadership of Junichiro Koizumi, until it was dealt one of its most serious defeats in the summer of 2007. In that election, the LDP lost control of the Diet's upper house, which is now run by the Democratic Party of Japan and other opposition parties. *Chin Music:* Through its first two decades, the LDP was helped by the Central Intelligence Agency of the US, which spent millions of dollars to help its candidates get elected and keep left-leaning politicians from winning. For more on this story, first reported by *The New York Times,* check out the Japan Policy Research Institute site and the work of Chalmers Johnson, Norbert A. Schlei and Michael Schaller here: http://www.jpri.org/publications/workingpapers/wp11.html

DEMOCRATIC PARTY OF JAPAN — The leading opposition party in Japan, headed by Ichiro Ozawa. It has controlled the upper house with its smaller coalition parties since July 2007. The party was established in 1998 when four opposition parties united to take on the ruling Liberal Democratic Party. While the DPJ is often described as "centrist," it is more of a mixed bag, with both liberal and conservative members, much like the American Democratic Party. *Chin Music:* The first Diet member of European ancestry, Marutei Tsurunen (formerly Martti Turunen of Lieksa, Finland), is a member of the DPJ. He has held public office on and off since 1992 and wrote a hit book in Japanese whose title translates to *Here Comes the Blue-Eyed Assemblyman.*

RECHALLENGE SOCIETY — A Japanese-English catchphrase that Shinzo Abe was fond of repeating when he was prime minister. The term means challenging oneself more than once, or picking yourself up by your bootstraps.

JAPAN'S CONSTITUTION — The Constitution was written and promulgated in November 1946, then officially enacted in 1947. Here is the preamble in its entirety:

We, the Japanese people, acting through our duly elected representatives in the National Diet, determined that we shall secure for ourselves and our posterity the fruits of peaceful cooperation with all nations and the blessings of liberty throughout this land, and resolved that never again shall we be visited with the horrors of war through the action of government, do proclaim that sovereign power resides with the people and do firmly establish this Constitution. Government is a sacred trust of the people, the authority for which is derived from the people, the powers of which are exercised by the representatives of the people, and the benefits of which are enjoyed by the people. This is a universal principle of mankind upon which this Constitution is founded. We reject and revoke all constitutions, laws, ordinances and rescripts in conflict herewith.

We, the Japanese people, desire peace for all time and are deeply conscious of the high ideals controlling human relationship, and we have determined to preserve our security and existence, trusting in the justice and faith of the peace-loving peoples of the world. We desire to occupy an honored place in an international society striving for the preservation of peace and the banishment of tyranny and slavery, oppression and intolerance for all time from the earth. We recognize that all peoples of the world have the right to live in peace, free from fear and want.

We believe that no nation is responsible to itself alone, but that laws of political morality are universal and that obedience to such laws is incumbent upon all nations who would sustain their own sovereignty and justify their sovereign relationship with other nations.

We, the Japanese people, pledge our national honor to accomplish these high ideals and purposes with all our resources.

The Constitution then outlines the role of the emperor ("Article 1: The Emperor shall be the symbol of the State and of the unity of the people, deriving his position from the will of the people with whom resides sovereign power."), the nation's renunciation of war ("Article 9: [T]he Japanese people forever renounce war as a sovereign right of the nation and the threat or use of force as means of settling international disputes.") and the rights and duties of the Japanese people ("Article 13: All of the people shall be respected as individuals. Their right to life, liberty and the pursuit of happiness shall, to the extent that it does not interfere with the public welfare, be the supreme consideration in legislation and in other governmental affairs.") It also outlines the structure of Japan's parliamentary democracy, judiciary and financial system.

Chapter 3: THE POSTWAR CHOICE: WHAT COULD HAVE BEEN

NOBUSUKE KISHI — Served as the fifty-sixth and fifty-seventh prime minister of Japan in consecutive terms that ran from February 25, 1957, to July 19, 1960. Kishi went from class A war criminal to prime minister in an historical blink of an eye once the Americans decided to exonerate him. He pushed through a US-Japan Mutual Security Treaty near the end of 1959, which set off protests and riots in Tokyo. *Chin Music:* In 1979, Kishi was awarded the United Nations Peace Medal with Ryoichi Sasakawa, another war criminal and self-proclaimed fascist who idolized Mussolini. Sasakawa's wealth, made partly through plundering China during the war and later in motor boat races and shipbuilding, provided the basis for today's Nippon Foundation.

YASUHIRO NAKASONE — Served three consecutive terms as Japan's seventy-first, seventy-second and seventy-third prime minister from November 27, 1982, to November 6, 1987. Like his counterparts Margaret Thatcher and Ronald Reagan in the West, Nakasone pushed the privatization of state-owned assets, especially the railroads, while in office. He was also known as an ardent nationalist. Nakasone and Reagan struck up their famous Ron-Yasu relationship during Nakasone's term as well. Nakasone was later implicated in the Recruit insider trading scandal, in which he and other Liberal Democratic Party politicians were accused of receiving discounted shares of a Recruit subsidiary along with a no-interest loan to buy those shares. *Chin Music:* Nakasone bought into the idea that the Japanese were a superior race. During his premiership, he made the following controversial statement: "So high is the level of education in our country that Japan's is an intelligent society. Our average score is much higher than those of countries like the US. There are many blacks, Puerto Ricans and Mexicans in America. In consequence the average score over there is exceedingly low."

ICHIRO HATOYAMA — Served three consecutive terms as Japan's fifty-second, fifty-third and fifty-fourth prime minister from December 10, 1954, to December 23, 1956, when he was forced to resign because of illness. He restored diplomatic ties to the Soviet Union and released some of Japan's war criminals. Yukio Hatoyama of the Democratic Party of Japan is Ichiro's grandson. *Chin Music:* Hatoyama flew to Moscow despite being gravely ill in 1956 to sign the Soviet-Japanese declaration officially ending a state of war between the two countries. Russian sculptor Zurab Tsereteli created a statue of Ichiro Hatoyama in 2007 that stands in Tokyo today.

TANZAN ISHIBASHI — Served as Japan's fifty-fifth prime minister from December 23, 1956, to February 25, 1957. Ishibashi's term was cut short because of illness. He had pledged to establish diplomatic relations with China but stepped down before he could fulfill that pledge. His resignation cleared the way for the more militant Nobusuke Kishi, who Ishibashi opposed.

SHIGERU YOSHIDA — Served as Japan's forty-fifth prime minister from May 22, 1946, to May 24, 1947. Later he served four consecutive terms as Japan's forty-eighth through fifty-first prime minister from October 15, 1948, to December 10, 1954. Yoshida was a pro-American and pro-British politician despite his work furthering imperialist causes before and during the war. Yoshida was at the helm as Japan began to rebuild its economy. *Chin Music:* Yoshida's grandson, Taro Aso, is a prominent member of the Liberal Democratic Party and served as foreign minister under Junichiro Koizumi. He is perhaps best known in the West for saying while serving as minister for economics and fiscal policy, "I think the best country is one in which rich Jews feel like living."

TREATY OF MUTUAL COOPERATION AND SECURITY — Signed by the US and Japan in January 1960, this treaty set Japan firmly on the side of the US in the Cold War, solidifying the security relationship between the two countries. The treaty bitterly divided Japan and led to rioting in the streets. When the Liberal Democratic Party members tried to enter the Diet to approve the bill, members of the Japan Socialist Party physically detained them until police arrived on the scene and dragged away the socialists. The riots by students and trade unions that ensued kept then President Dwight D. Eisenhower from visiting Japan and led to the eventual resignation of Prime Minister Nobosuke Kishi, a staunch proponent of the treaty.

SAN FRANCISCO PEACE TREATY — Signed on September 8, 1951, in San Francisco by representatives of forty-nine countries, this treaty made the end of World War II official. Its official name is the Treaty of Peace with Japan.

SECURITY TREATY OF 1951 — Once the San Francisco Peace Treaty was signed, Japan was officially disarmed and unable to defend itself. The Security Treaty of 1951 established that "Japan desires, as a provisional arrangement for its defense, that the United States of America should maintain armed forces of its own in and about Japan so as to deter armed attack upon Japan." This provisional arrangement became semipermanent with the 1960 signing of the Treaty of Mutual Cooperation and Security.

MORIHIRO HOSOKAWA — Served as the seventy-ninth prime minister of Japan from August 9, 1993, to April 28, 1994. He was at the head of a coalition that took power from the Liberal Democratic Party for the first time since the LDP was formed in 1955. Hosokawa began as a member of the LDP, but he formed the Japan New Party in 1992 because he was fed up with the corruption of the ruling party. His election brought a sense of excitement and hope to Japanese politics that turned out to be short-lived. He apologized for Japan's role in World War II, which he called a "war of aggression, a mistaken war," becoming the first Japanese leader to do so. But he was soon after brought down by allegations that he had received a bribe of nearly $1 million from Sagawa Kyuubin, a parcel delivery company.

EISAKU SATO — Served three consecutive terms as the sixty-first, sixty-second and sixty-third prime minister of Japan from November 9, 1964, to July 7, 1972, making him the longest-serving postwar premier. In 1969, Sato negotiated the return of Okinawa to Japan with then US President Richard Nixon.

PRESS CLUB SYSTEM — Japanese journalism runs on a system where certified reporters work out of a press club attached to a ministry or government body. Those reporters—and those reporters alone—have access to certain information and sources within the governmental body. The press often censors itself so as not to incur the wrath of a government body, which could have the media organization's press club credentials rescinded. This sort of distribution of information has been called the "information cartel" model.

Chapter 4: LIFE AFTER BUSH

KIICHI MIYAZAWA — Served as Japan's seventy-eighth prime minister from November 5, 1991, to August 9, 1993. He held many government posts, including finance minister in the mid 1980s, before ascending to premier. He pushed for the Self-Defense Forces to be allowed to go overseas to aid humanitarian crises and he negotiated a major trade pact with the US that focused on reducing Japan's trade surplus and opening Japanese markets to US competition. He resigned after losing a no-confidence vote in 1993, ending what had been thirty-eight consecutive years of Liberal Democratic Party rule. Miyazawa died on June 28, 2007. *Chin Music:* Despite his political pedigree and impressive resume, Miyazawa will probably always be remembered by Americans as the premier George H. W. Bush threw up on at a banquet in Japan in 1992.

US-JAPAN REGULATORY REFORM AND COMPETITION POLICY INITIATIVE — This initiative was formed by President George W.

Bush and Prime Minister Junichiro Koizumi in 2001. Every fall, the two governments exchange reform recommendations. Here is a brief sampling of the most recent round of recommendations that the US made in October 2007:

Medical Devices and Pharmaceuticals

◆ End the lag in the introduction of innovative medical devices and drugs by streamlining reviews and approval.

◆ Nutritional supplements: Create a new category for foods that allow ingredient-specific claims; provide meaningful opportunities for industry input during the development of health food safety regulations; shorten approval times for new additives.

◆ Improve and stabilize economic returns for advanced patented drugs during their patent life or exclusivity period to reflect accurately their level of innovation and the financial risks taken to develop them.

Privatization

◆ Ensure [the new postal financial institutions] do not actively leverage their government ties to secure new advantages ... create a level playing field in Japan's banking and insurance sectors before postal financial institutions are permitted to introduce new lending services, underwrite new or altered insurance products and originate non-principal-guaranteed investment products.

◆ Provide meaningful and timely opportunities for private sector interested parties to exchange views with relevant Government of Japan officials on matters pertaining to Japan Post reforms that may affect the private sector.

Chapter 5: ANTAGONIZING CHINA: THE FAVORITE SPORT OF JAPAN'S NEOCONS

NEW KOMEITO — This political party is backed and founded by members of Soka Gakkai, Japan's largest lay Buddhist organization. New Komeito is a junior coalition partner with the Liberal Democratic Party; together, they control the lower house. *Chin Music:* New Komeito's devoted religious followers have proved easier to organize and mobilize than other Japanese voting blocs. In 2003, *Time* magazine wrote this about the party: "Because of its religious ties, which help create an obedient rank and file, the New Komeito has one of the last great vote-gathering machines in Japan. Political analysts estimate that New Komeito delivers between twenty thousand and thirty thousand votes in every major constituency (and many elections have been decided by only a few thousand ballots). Some eighty percent of LDP candidates who received a New Komeito endorsement this time around were elected. In contrast, fifty-five percent of LDP candidates without the New Komeito imprimatur won their races."

KOUKI KOBAYASHI — A former Diet member who lost his lower-house seat in Junichiro Koizumi's big September 2005 electoral victory, Kobayashi writes a blog at http://ameblo.jp/kobaya-shikouki/ (Japanese only). *Chin Music:* Kobayashi's nickname is Koba-chan.

YOSHIHISA KOMORI — Editor at large of the *Sankei Shimbun*, a national newspaper in Japan. He has held posts in London, China and most recently Washington DC. He has written many books, several of which are critical of China and the China-Japan relationship (*Japan and China: Illusion of Friendship*, 2002; *Japan-China Relationship Reconsidered*, 2001, for example). *Chin Music:*

Noted Japan scholar Steve Clemons called Komori "sort of the Rush Limbaugh of Japanese journalism." Komori was a staunch defender of former Prime Minister Shinzo Abe. He wrote an editorial in *The New York Times* calling Abe "thoroughly modern and straightforward." On Abe's stance toward China, he wrote:

"A significant part of Japan's baggage over the last sixty-one years is related to its activities in China during the war. Although Japan accepted all judgments of the Tokyo War Crimes Tribunal and other regional war tribunals, and signed the San Francisco Peace Treaty, China in particular has aggressively pushed viewpoints that inflate and contradict those judgments. For years, Japan's government stayed quiet to avoid denunciations of 'whitewashing.'

"Mr. Abe, while openly acknowledging and expressing remorse for Japan's wartime mistakes and atrocities, was among the first politicians to question government silence on these escalating emotional and uncorroborated claims, and to point out that Japan's postwar prime ministers have formally apologized to China more than twenty times for Japan's wartime transgressions. Mr. Abe has said one of the new government's priorities is improved relations with China, but noted that 'it takes two to reconcile.' He looks forward to a China that can accept today's democratic Japan."

SANKEI SHIMBUN — A national newspaper with a combined morning and evening circulation of about 2.7 million, making it Japan's sixth largest paper. Wikipedia describes the paper's editorial views as "nationalist, anti-communist, conservative and pro-United States." It is part of the Fujisankei Communications Group.

TERUMASA NAKANISHI — A professor of international politics at Kyoto University. The sixty-one-year-old academic is also a graduate of Kyoto University; he did graduate work at the University of Cambridge. *Chin Music:* Nakanishi argues that the threat from North Korea provides Japan with enough reason to arm itself with nuclear weapons. He and literary critic Kazuya Fukuda wrote in *Voice* magazine in early 2003: "The best way for Japan to avoid being the target of North Korean nuclear missiles is for the prime minister to declare without delay that Japan will arm itself with nuclear weapons."

YOSHIKO SAKURAI — A journalist and TV reporter, Sakurai is a graduate of the University of Hawaii at Manoa. She began her journalism career with the *Christian Science Monitor* and later became a fixture on Nippon Television's news programs. Now she spends her time writing books. Her most famous book, *AIDS Crime: The Tragedy of Hemophiliacs*, broke the story of how HIV-tainted blood products were not screened by the Japanese government, leading to the infection of forty percent of Japan's hemophiliacs. *Chin Music:* While a writer in *The Japan Times* once breathlessly called Sakurai "Japan's bravest and most responsible journalist," she is not without controversy. In fact, she's become the right wing's front woman on the issue of the Japanese military harboring sex slaves during World War II, sweetly telling the world that the claims "are not based on fact." She was one of a group of academics and lawmakers who took a full-page ad out in *The Washington Post* in 2007 that accused the "comfort women," as the sex slaves are euphemistically called, of distorting history. The ad absolved the Japanese army, according to a McClatchy Newspapers report, which also quoted US Rep. Tom Lantos saying in response to the ad: "The advertisement suggests that these women, who were forcibly and repeatedly raped by soldiers, were engaged, and I quote, in 'licensed prostitution that was commonplace around the world at the time.' This is a ludicrous assertion totally counter to the facts."

YOSHIYUKI KASAI — Chairman of the Central Japan Railway Co., he was a key player in the privatization of the Japanese National Railways. He's the author of the English-language book *Japanese National Railways: Its Breakup and Privatization.*

HIDETSUGU YAGI — A professor of law at the Takasaki City University of Economics and the president of the Japanese Society for History Textbook Reform, a conservative group that wants to build a sense of patriotism in Japanese classrooms. The group has been accused of trying to whitewash Japan's history to downplay its actions in World War II.

YASUO FUKUDA — Serving as Japan's ninety-first prime minister of Japan as of this writing. He took the helm on September 26, 2007, after Shinzo Abe resigned, and has tried to stake out a middle ground diplomatically and politically.

SOKA GAKKAI — Japan's largest lay Buddhist organization. It is a branch of Nichiren Buddhism that dates back to the 1930s. The organization is run by Daisuke Ikeda, the honorary president and head of Soka Gakkai International, which boasts twelve million members. *Chin Music:* Although it is widely held that Soka Gakkai has great influence over the New Komeito political party, the party itself denies this on its website:

In summary, the Soka Gakkai is a constituency that has provided electoral endorsement to the party until today. The relation between the two entities is no different from that of a political party and any civil group — such as a labor union, for example — that endorses the party, and it has been established as being constitutionally legitimate.

In Japan, moreover, major groups or companies, including religious organizations, have routinely endorsed political parties and/or candidates. To further clarify the nature of the relationship, in 1970, Komeito and the Soka Gakkai severed all organizational affiliation. (Prior to that time it was possible for an individual to hold appointments in both organizations.) The Soka Gakkai has not provided any degree of oversight to the Komei Party or its current successor, New Komeito, in terms of personnel, management or administration, since then. Nor has there ever been any financial affiliation between the Soka Gakkai and the political party since the latter's launch in 1964.

DENTSU — The world's largest advertising agency and an immensely powerful social and political force in Japan. It often runs the ad campaigns of competitors in the same markets. For example, it simultaneously ran the campaigns for three competitors in the mobile phone market: NTT DoCoMo, KDDI and SoftBank. *Chin Music:* Dentsu is so powerful that it plays by different rules. Junichiro Koizumi's government offered the agency a no-bid contract to set up fake town hall meetings around Japan. The meetings were supposed to let citizens air their views on postal privatization and other key issues, but of course, most of the questions and comments were made by people who were paid to attend the meetings and ask pro-government questions. Dentsu was a close adviser to Koizumi from the beginning of his term in 2001. The fake town hall meetings went on for years before they were exposed. Despite the gravity of the scandal, Dentsu's role was often left out of news reports or forgotten altogether, and the mammoth ad agency emerged almost completely unscathed.

HIDENAO NAKAGAWA — A lower house lawmaker and an influential member of the Liberal Democratic Party. He served as secretary-general of the party under Shinzo Abe. *Chin Music:* Nakagawa was forced to resign as chief cabinet secretary under Prime Minister Yoshiro Mori when the weekly entertainment magazine *Focus* exposed an extramarital affair that he later admitted to. He also sued the mistress and magazine for libel and won.

SHINTARO ISHIHARA — The governor of Tokyo and author of the 1991 best-seller *The Japan That Can Say No.* Ishihara is an outspoken nationalist who has made many disparaging remarks about China and Korea and who is a regular visitor to Yasukuni Shrine, a Shinto shrine dedicated to the soldiers who died for the emperor. As governor, he has imposed new taxes on banks' gross profit (as opposed to net profit) and cut spending on transportation. *Chin Music:* "I hate Mickey Mouse," Ishihara was quoted as saying in 2006. "He has nothing like the unique sensibility that Japan has. The Japanese are inherently skilled at visual expression and detailed work." Around the same time, popular novelist Haruki Murakami, talking about his fears of Japanese nationalism, had this to say about the Tokyo governor: "Ishihara is a very dangerous man. He is an agitator. He hates China."

COMMUNIST PARTY — The Japanese Communist Party was founded in 1922 and was immediately made illegal by the Japanese government. It was the only party in Japan that opposed Japan's involvement in World War II, and it is the only party today that claims the Japan-US security arrangement keeps Japan from being a truly independent nation. The party distanced itself from the Soviet Union, even saying it welcomed the end of imperialism when the USSR collapsed. Today it retains just a smattering of legislators in the two houses of the Diet but is still quite active in local politics.

Chapter 7: THE BATTLE FOR IWAKUNI CITY

US MILITARY REALIGNMENT PLAN — A 2006 agreement between Japan and the US on reconfiguration of the US forces called for transferring an aircraft carrier air wing of about sixty planes based at the US Naval Air Facility Atsugi, Kanagawa, to Iwakuni by 2014. Also, a squadron of 12 KC-130 tankers are to be transferred to Iwakuni from Okinawa. The number of marines and dependents in Iwakuni was about 5,400 at the time of this writing. Once the transfer is completed, the number will almost double.

TAKEMASA MORIYA — The former vice defense minister was arrested along with his wife in November 2007 for allegedly taking bribes from a former Yamada Corp, executive. As vice defense minister, Moriya was the top bureaucrat in the Defense Ministry (the minister is appointed, making the vice-minister the top bureaucratic post). The couple was accused of taking bribes worth millions of yen in the form of golf outings, loans to repay family debts and payments to the Moriyas' daughter. Prosecutors argue that at least four million yen in payments were considered bribes although the couple allegedly received much more than that.

KATSUSUKE IHARA — The former mayor of Iwakuni City, he stepped down in 2008 to seek a mandate for his views, especially his staunch opposition to the US military base expansion being planned in Iwakuni. He lost a very close election, but largely because he was the victim of a smear campaign that alleged he was the reason for the city's financial woes. He has since formed a citizens' group, is considering forming a new political party and has vowed to fight on against the expansion of the US military presence in Iwakuni and elsewhere.

ROKA TOKUTOMI — A novelist who lived around the 1900s and achieved modest success with books like *The Cuckoo* and *Footprints in the Snow*. *Chin Music:* Tokutomi traveled to Russia to meet one of his heroes, Leo Tolstoy, and seemed profoundly moved by the meeting. Like his Russian counterpart, Tokutomi retired to the country to lead a simple peasant life.

SHIGERU ISHIBA — Minister of defense under current Prime Minister Yasuo Fukuda. He was a strong supporter of having Japanese troops sent to Iraq. *Chin Music:* Ishiba took a little heat at the end of 2007 for his stated belief in UFOs and his ponderings of how the Japanese military should handle a chance encounter. He was quoted by Bloomberg News as saying, "If they descended, saying 'People of the Earth, let's make friends,' it would not be considered an urgent, unjust attack on our country ... How can we convey our intentions if they don't understand what we are saying?"

COMFORT WOMEN — A euphemism for the sex slaves held in brothels patronized by Japanese soldiers during World War II. *Chin Music:* In early 2007, the comfort women issue jumped back onto the front pages of the world's newspapers when then Prime Minister Shinzo Abe declared, "The fact is, there is no evidence to prove there was coercion." This is a common argument among Japan's right wingers. There is no proof of coercion, so this issue really isn't about sexual slavery and rape, they argue. And of course, they're wrong. Documents found in 1992 show that Japanese authorities urged the establishment of brothels to stop the troops from raping and terrorizing local women.

YOMIURI SHIMBUN — One of the world's largest newspapers and the most widely read paper in Japan, it has a combined morning and evening circulation of more than fourteen million readers. It has a right-of-center bent.

Chapter 8: STOPPING THE KOIZUMI REVOLUTION

OCCUPATION — The Allied Powers, led by the US, occupied Japan from the end of World War II in 1945 until 1952, when the San Francisco Peace Treaty went into effect and Japan officially became an independent nation.

Chapter 9: AMERICANIZING JAPAN'S ECONOMY

"HUNDRED MILLION MIDDLE CLASS" — The phrase is used to connote the sense that at one point just about all of Japan was considered middle class. Japan has a population of about 127 million people.

FEBRUARY 26TH INCIDENT — An attempted coup d'etats led by extreme nationalists within the Imperial Japanese Army against the Japanese government. The coup began on February 26, 1936, and lasted three days, during which time the radical kodo-ha faction took control of downtown Tokyo. There were nearly fifteen hundred troops involved in the attempted overthrow of the government. They claimed that they were fighting for the emperor to rid Japan of venal politicians. But Emperor Showa, then known by the name Hirohito, was incensed at the murders that ensued and demanded the rebellion be quashed. By February 29, many of the rebel troops had deserted. In the end, two officers of the rebellion committed ritual suicide and the remainder were arrested. *Chin Music:* One of novelist Yukio Mishima's most famous short stories, "Patriotism," was based on this February 26th incident. He also released a short film by the same title that depicts a rebel lieutenant committing hara-kiri after the coup had failed. Mishima also died by ritual suicide in 1970 at the Ground Self-Defense Force regional headquarters in Tokyo's Ichigaya district. Although Mishima's wife was said to have destroyed all the copies of the film after his suicide, in 2005, a negative of the film was found.

US FIREBOMBINGS — Firebombings of Japanese cities by American troops occurred several times during World War II, but the worst night was March 10, 1945, when an estimated eighty thousand to 100,000 were killed in Tokyo, which is more than were killed when the atomic bomb was dropped on Nagasaki.

Chapter 10: EXPLOITED & ENTRAPPED

FUNDAMENTAL LAW OF EDUCATION — This law sets the standards for Japan's education system. It was created in March 1947 and remained as is until 2006, when the Liberal Democratic Party and its coalition partner New Komeito pushed through revisions to the law (see EDUCATION REFORM BILL in chapter sixteen notes).

The original law stated that the purpose of Japanese education was the full development of personality. Article 1 states: "Education shall aim at the full development of personality, striving for the rearing of the people, sound in mind and body, who shall love truth and justice, esteem individual value, respect labor and have a deep sense of responsibility, and be imbued with the independent spirit, as builders of a peaceful state and society."

DEFENSE MINISTRY — The Defense Agency was upgraded to the Defense Ministry in January 2007, raising its status to a cabinet-level organization.

CONSTITUTIONAL REVISIONS — Refers to efforts to revise Article 9 of the Japan Constitution, which states: "1. Aspiring sincerely to an international peace based on justice and order, the Japanese people forever renounce war as a sovereign right of the nation and the threat or use of force as means of settling international disputes; 2. In order to accomplish the aim of the preceding paragraph, land, sea, and air forces, as well as other war potential, will never be maintained. The right of belligerency of the state will not be recognized." Those in favor of revisions argue that Japan's military should be on equal footing with those of other countries.

Chapter 11: EMERGENCE OF THE WORKING POOR

SHUKAN ECONOMIST — A weekly business magazine.

BUNGEI SHUNJU — A popular monthly magazine that deals with politics, social issues and culture.

NHK — Known in English as Japan Broadcasting Corp., NHK is the largest public broadcaster of television and radio in Japan. It offers a diverse menu of programs from news to entertainment. *Chin Music:* Perhaps the most famous employee in NHK's history is Iva Ikuko Toguri, known by her radio name Orphan Ann, but more widely known by a name she never uttered on air, Tokyo Rose. Toguri was picked out of the NHK typist pool to become a radio DJ in 1943. Her fascinating, tragic tale and some audio files of her infamous broadcasts can be found on this website: http://www.earthstation1.com/Tokyo_Rose.html

SALARYMEN — A Japanese-English word used to refer to white-collar workers, but with a more sad-sack tone than "white-collar worker" implies.

ASAHI SHIMBUN — The second most widely read daily newspaper in Japan, after the *Yomiuri Shimbun*. The *Asahi Shimbun* has a combined morning and evening circulation of about twelve million readers. Editorially it leans a little bit to the left.

Chapter 12: THE ARROGANCE AND MYOPIA OF KEIDANREN

KEIDANREN — Nippon Keidanren is its official name and the official English translation is Japan Business Federation. The group represents big business in Japan. It says its mission is "to accelerate growth of Japan's and the world's economy and to strengthen corporations to create additional value to transform the Japanese economy into one that is sustainable and driven by the private sector." Keidanren's membership list reads like a who's who of corporate Japan. The group is known for being very conservative.

FUJIO MITARAI — Chairman of both Nippon Keidanren and Canon Inc.

COUNCIL ON ECONOMIC AND FISCAL POLICY — This group was established as part of the cabinet office in 2001 to help reorganize Japan's ministries. The council, populated by a mix of politicians and corporate executives, is also supposed to file reports and opinions on economic matters. Prime Minister Yasuo Fukuda presides over the group.

NIHON KEIZAI SHIMBUN — Japan's largest economic daily newspaper. Often called Japan's *Wall Street Journal*. The morning and evening editions have a combined circulation of more than three million readers.

Chapter 13: POSTAL PRIVATIZATION NIGHTMARES

MASAHARU IKUTA — President of Japan Post from 2003 to 2007. Ikuta led the agency up until it was privatized later in 2007. Ikuta was CEO of Mitsui OSK, a major shipping line, before taking over the massive postal agency. *Chin Music:* In August 2005, consumer advocate Ralph Nader wrote the following letter to Ikuta:

Mr. Masaharu Ikuta
Japan Post
1-3-2 Kasumigaseki, Chiyoda-ku
Tokyo 100-8798
Japan

Dear Mr. Masaharu Ikuta:

For many years I have been aware of the high level of mail and financial services provided by the Japanese post office. Mail service is accurate and efficient, and post offices are located in even the smallest towns.

It should be remembered that Japan's postal savings system is not only a convenience; it has helped extend financial services broadly and assisted efforts to stabilize and stimulate the economy for years through public works projects. Additionally, postal employees are well known for looking after their communities. The International Herald Tribune *has rightly reported that Japanese postmasters are "pillars of the community."*

However, despite its record of success, Prime Minister Junichiro Koizumi has continually insisted on pushing for postal privatization. As a citizen of the United States, I find it troubling that he is supported by the US Trade Representative and the US Chamber of Commerce, organizations that want privatization for an obvious combination of ideological and self-interested commercial motivations. Koizumi's demands are only supported by twenty-four percent of the Japanese people. The Japanese public understands that privatization would lead to a reduction in postal services and possibly disenfranchisement. Elimination of the postal monopoly in such nations as Sweden and New Zealand has led to the closure of half of these nation's post offices, and Argentina's venture into postal privatization was such an abject failure that it was recently renationalized.

Instead of pushing ill-advised privatization schemes, US policy makers should be looking to Japan for pointers on successfully running a postal service, including establishing a postal savings program for millions of Americans who cannot afford or are denied banking services.

Sincerely,
Ralph Nader
CC: Prime Minister Junichiro Koizumi

JAPAN POST — The name of the Japanese postal system from 2003 until its privatization began in 2007. It was Japan's largest employer, with more than 400,000 employees, and the largest savings bank in the world, with about ¥224 trillion (more than two trillion dollars) in savings accounts and another ¥126 trillion in life insurance policies. It was a massive and quite well run organization for the most part, but it was privatized in fall 2007 and is now run by various Japan Post Group companies.

KYODO — A major Japanese news service. It is run as a nonprofit cooperative similar to the Associated Press. Its news is distributed to most major media organizations in Japan.

HEIZO TAKENAKA — An economist who served in Junichiro Koizumi's cabinet as minister of state for privatization of the postal services. He also served as minister of internal affairs and communications. He teaches economics at Keio University. *Chin Music:* A privatization zealot, Takenaka had his eye on the Japan Public Broadcasting Corp. (NHK) after his work on the postal system, but even Junichiro Koizumi resisted the urge to privatize the public broadcaster.

KAN-I POST OFFICES — These "convenient" post offices are just little windows located in stores and small retail shops where people can buy stamps and mail letters. They are being phased out as part of postal privatization.

Chapter 14: AMERICA'S NEXT TARGET: JAPAN'S MEDICAL SYSTEM

MEDICAL SYSTEM REFORM LAW — As Japanese society rapidly ages, reforms to the medical system have led to higher co-pays for the elderly, pressure on hospitals to reduce the length of hospital stays and numerical targets for the reduction of lifestyle diseases such as diabetes. Elderly people will have to pay more for their hospital rooms and meals as a result of these reforms. Also, the reforms reduce the amount of hospital beds reserved for elderly care, forcing more senior citizens to be treated at home. The Health Ministry claims these and other related medical reforms will save the government eight trillion yen by 2025.

VULTURE-CAPITAL FUNDS — Refers to funds used to swoop down on the carcass of a dying company and pick over the remains. Commonly used in Japan to refer to foreign investors looking to capitalize on weaknesses in the Japanese economy.

Chapter 16: PATRIOTISM AND US INFLUENCE IN THE CLASSROOM

EDUCATIONAL REFORM BILL — This bill was enacted as law in December 2006, changing the Fundamental Law of Education for the first time since it was created in 1947. The revisions, pushed through the Diet by the Liberal Democratic Party and its coalition partner New Komeito, added seven articles to the original law's eleven. One of the more contentious additions is a phrase—"cultivating an attitude which respects tradition and culture and love of the nation and homeland"—meant to increase patriotism in schools. Also, while the original law said, "The people shall all be given equal opportunities of receiving education according to their ability, and they shall not be subject to educational discrimination on account of race, creed, sex, social status, economic position, or family origin," the revised law has dropped the word "equal."

GENERAL HEADQUARTERS (GHQ) — Used in Japan to refer to the Supreme Commander of the Allied Powers (SCAP), the leader of the Allied Occupation of Japan, which was General Douglas MacArthur.

LIBERAL PARTY — This political party, led by Shigeru Yoshida, merged with the Democratic Party in 1955 to create the Liberal Democratic Party. Not to be confused with the Liberal Party founded in 1998 by Ichiro Ozawa and Hirohisa Fujii, which is now defunct, having merged into the Democratic Party of Japan.

DEMOCRATIC PARTY — Also called the Japan Democratic Party, this political party, led by Ichiro Hatoyama, merged with the Liberal Party in 1955 to create the Liberal Democratic Party. The two parties decided to merge to take on the Socialist Party.

SOCIALIST PARTY — Known at the time as the Japan Socialist Party. For more than half a century since the end of World War II, the party was Japan's main opposition party. In 1995 it decided to rename itself the Social Democratic Party. As the Democratic Party of Japan's star has risen, making it the leading opposition party, the SDP has shrunk to a small party that holds just several seats.

IMPERIAL UNIVERSITY SYSTEM — Japan established nine imperial universities between 1877 and 1939. The universities, which were run by the imperial government, are listed here with their current names in parentheses: Keijo Imperial University (disbanded), Kyoto Imperial University (Kyoto University), Kyushu Imperial University

(Kyushu University), Hokkaido Imperial University (Hokkaido University), Nagoya Imperial University (Nagoya University), Osaka Imperial University (Osaka University), Taihoku Imperial University (National Taiwan University), Tohoku Imperial University (Tohoku University) and Tokyo Imperial University (the University of Tokyo).

NATIONAL UNIVERSITY SYSTEM — The imperial university system was turned into the national university system after World War II. See the previous entry for a list of the universities in the original imperial system.

PRESS CODE — The Supreme Allied Commander issued a Code for the Japanese Press on September 21, 1945. It laid down the rules for Japan's media:

1. *News must adhere strictly to the truth.*
2. *Nothing should be printed which might, directly or indirectly, disturb the public tranquility.*
3. *There shall be no false or destructive criticism of the Allied Powers.*
4. *There shall be no destructive criticism of the Allied Occupation and nothing which might invite mistrust or resentment of those troops.*
5. *There shall be no mention or discussion of Allied troop movements unless such movements have been officially released.*
6. *News stories must be factually written and completely devoid of editorial opinion.*
7. *News stories shall not be colored to conform with any propaganda line.*
8. *Minor details of a news story must not be over-emphasized to stress or develop any propaganda line.*

9. *No news story shall be distorted by the omission of pertinent facts or details.*

10. *In the make-up of the newspaper, no news story shall be given undue prominence for the purpose of establishing or developing any propaganda line.*

Chapter 17: CONSTITUTIONAL REFORMS ON AN AMERICAN TIMETABLE

SELF-DEFENSE FORCES — Officially known as the Japan Self-Defense Forces, this is Japan's military. They have slowly but steadily expanded their reach. In the first few decades after World War II, they were not allowed to leave Japan. Then they were allowed to take part in international peacekeeping operations, and under Junichiro Koizumi's leadership, the forces offered support to US troops engaged in the Iraq War. *Chin Music:* Another sign of the increasingly powerful role of the military in Japan is that what was once the Japan Defense Agency was upgraded to the Defense Ministry in January 2007.

Chapter 19: FROM THE CLASH OF CIVILIZATIONS TO AN ERA OF LESSENED TENSIONS

TOMIICHI MURAYAMA — Served as Japan's eighty-first prime minister from June 30, 1994, to January 11, 1996. Murayama was the head of the Social Democratic Party, formerly the Japan Socialist Party. As the first Socialist prime minister in postwar history, Murayama apologized for Japanese atrocities in World War II. Yet Murayama was a Socialist premier in an odd coalition with two conservative parties, the Liberal Democratic Party and New Party Sakigake. The coalition gave him little actual power.

RYUTARO HASHIMOTO — Served consecutive terms as Japan's eighty-second and eighty-third prime minister from January 11, 1996, to July 30, 1998. He died on July 1, 2006.

KEIZO OBUCHI — Served as Japan's eighty-fourth prime minister from July 30, 1998, to April 5, 2000. His term came to an end when he suffered a serious stroke and later died. *Chin Music:* Obuchi threw out the first pitch at a baseball game in Wrigley Field in May 1999. The catcher was Sammy Sosa of the Chicago Cubs. The pitch barely made it to the plate, and Sosa had to lunge to catch it. The editors apologize for that completely superfluous baseball reference.

ABOUT
THE AUTHOR

Minoru Morita is a world-renowned political commentator and activist who has written dozens of books on Japanese society and politics. He is also the founder of the Morita Research Institute, a progressive think tank.

Morita was born on October 23, 1932, in Ito, Shizuoka Prefecture. He served briefly in the Japanese military during his middle school years right at the end of World War II.

Morita graduated from the engineering department of the University of Tokyo. He worked as director of the major publishing company Nippon Hyoron-sha in the 1960s as well as editor of its main economic magazine before becoming an independent political analyst in the 1970s.

As his career took off, Morita became a fixture on Japanese TV, at times donning a man's kimono as he doled out his daily political insights.

However, after he began criticizing the then popular Prime Minister Junichiro Koizumi in 2005, his TV appearances began to dry up. Some media watchers say that Morita may also have been punished for his outspoken criticism of Dentsu Inc., Japan's advertising behemoth.

Once TV was no longer an option, the indefatigable Morita concentrated on getting his message to the Japanese people via his daily website postings (http://www.pluto.dti.ne.jp/~mor97512/) and through a steady stream of about three hundred public lectures a year. He also continued to be quoted often by the foreign press.

In early 2008, Morita unveiled his plan to launch a chain of learning institutes called Morita Juku to inform Japanese citizens and better equip them for coming political and societal changes. The institute began operations in spring 2008.

TYPOGRAPHIC PARTICULARS

body face
FF META SERIF
ERIK SPIEKERMANN,
CHRISTIAN SCHWARTZ
& KRIS SOWERSBY

headline sans
FLAMA SEMICONDENSED
MÁRIO FELICIANO

misc display serif
FEIJOA DISPLAY
KRIS SOWERSBY

.